UNDERSTANDING
DRUGS

Steroids and Other Performance-Enhancing Drugs

TITLES IN THE *UNDERSTANDING DRUGS* SERIES

Steroids and Other Performance-Enhancing Drugs

SUELLEN MAY

CONSULTING EDITOR
DAVID J. TRIGGLE, PH.D.
University Professor
School of Pharmacy and Pharmaceutical Sciences
State University of New York at Buffalo

CHELSEA HOUSE
An Infobase Learning Company

Steroids and Other Performance-Enhancing Drugs

Copyright © 2011 by Infobase Learning

Chelsea House
An imprint of Infobase Learning
132 West 31st Street
New York, NY 10001

Library of Congress Cataloging-in-Publication Data

May, Suellen.
  Steroids and other performance-enhancing drugs / Suellen May ; consulting editor, David J. Triggle.
    p. cm. — (Understanding drugs)
  Includes bibliographical references and index.
  ISBN-13: 978-1-60413-552-7 (hardcover : alk. paper)
  ISBN-10: 1-60413-552-2 (hardcover : alk. paper)   1. Anabolic steroids—Health aspects—Juvenile literature.   2. Doping in sports—Juvenile literature.   I. Triggle, D. J.   II. Title. III. Series.
  RC1230.M376 2011
  362.29—dc22   2011001012

Text design by Kerry Casey
Cover design by Alicia Post
Composition by Newgen North America
Cover printed by Yurchak Printing, Landisville, Pa.
Book printed and bound by Yurchak Printing, Landisville, Pa.
Date printed: June 2011
Printed in the United States of America

10 9 8 7 6 5 4 3 2 1

Contents

Foreword

THE USE AND ABUSE OF DRUGS

For thousands of years, humans have used a variety of sources with which to cure their ills, cast out devils, promote their well-being, relieve their misery, and control their fertility. Until the beginning of the twentieth century, the agents used were all of natural origin, including many derived from plants as well as elements such as antimony, sulfur, mercury, and arsenic. The sixteenth-century alchemist and physician Paracelsus used mercury and arsenic in his treatment of syphilis, worms, and other diseases that were common at that time; his cure rates, however, remain unknown. Many drugs used today have their origins in natural products. Antimony derivatives, for example, are used in the treatment of the nasty tropical disease leishmaniasis. These plant-derived products represent molecules that have been "forged in the crucible of evolution" and continue to supply the scientist with molecular scaffolds for new drug development.

Our story of modern drug discovery may be considered to start with the German physician and scientist Paul Ehrlich, often called the father of chemotherapy. Born in 1854, Ehrlich became interested in the ways in which synthetic dyes, then becoming a major product of the German fine chemical industry, could selectively stain certain tissues and components of cells. He reasoned that such dyes might form the basis for drugs that could interact selectively with diseased or foreign cells and organisms. One of Ehrlich's early successes was development of the arsenical "606"—patented under the name *Salvarsan*—as a treatment for syphilis. Ehrlich's goal was to create a "magic bullet," a drug that would target only the diseased cell or the invading disease-causing organism and have no effect on healthy cells and tissues. In this he was not successful, but his great research did lay the groundwork for the successes of the twentieth century, including the discovery of the sulfonamides and the antibiotic penicillin. The latter agent saved countless lives during World War II. Ehrlich, like many scientists, was an optimist. On the eve of World War I, he wrote, "Now that the liability to, and danger of, disease are to a large extent circumscribed—the efforts of chemotherapeutics are directed as far as possible to fill up the gaps left in this ring." As we shall see in the pages of this volume, it is neither the first nor the last time that science has proclaimed its victory over nature, only to have to see this optimism dashed in the light of some freshly emerging infection.

From these advances, however, has come the vast array of drugs that are available to the modern physician. We are increasingly close to Ehrlich's magic bullet: Drugs can now target very specific molecular defects in a number of cancers, and doctors today have the ability to investigate the human genome to more effectively match the drug and the patient. In the next one to two decades, it is almost certain that the cost of "reading" an individual genome will be sufficiently cheap that, at least in the developed world, such personalized medicines will become the norm. The development of such drugs, however, is extremely costly and raises significant social issues, including equity in the delivery of medical treatment.

The twenty-first century will continue to produce major advances in medicines and medicine delivery. Nature is, however, a resilient foe. Diseases and organisms develop resistance to existing drugs, and new drugs must constantly be developed. (This is particularly true for anti-infective and anticancer agents.) Additionally, new and more lethal forms of existing infectious diseases can develop rapidly. With the ease of global travel, these can spread from Timbuktu to Toledo in less than 24 hours and become pandemics. Hence the current concerns with avian flu. Also, diseases that have previously been dormant or geographically circumscribed may suddenly break out worldwide. (Imagine, for example, a worldwide pandemic of Ebola disease, with public health agencies totally overwhelmed.) Finally, there are serious concerns regarding the possibility of man-made epidemics occurring through the deliberate or accidental spread of disease agents—including manufactured agents, such as smallpox with enhanced lethality. It is therefore imperative that the search for new medicines continue.

All of us at some time in our life will take a medicine, even if it is only aspirin for a headache or to reduce cosmetic defects. For some individuals, drug use will be constant throughout life. As we age, we will likely be exposed to a variety of medications—from childhood vaccines to drugs to relieve pain caused by a terminal disease. It is not easy to get accurate and understandable information about the drugs that we consume to treat diseases and disorders. There are, of course, highly specialized volumes aimed at medical or scientific professionals. These, however, demand a sophisticated knowledge base and experience to be comprehended. Advertising on television is widely available but provides only fleeting information, usually about only a single drug and designed to market rather than inform. The intent of this series of books, **Understanding Drugs**, is to provide the lay reader with intelligent, readable, and accurate descriptions of drugs, why and how they are used, their limitations, their side effects, and their future. The series will discuss both *"treatment drugs"*—typically, but not exclusively, prescription drugs, that have well-established criteria of both efficacy and safety—and *"drugs of abuse"* that have pronounced pharmacological and physiological effects but that are considered, for a variety of reasons, not to be considered for therapeutic purposes. It is our hope that these books will provide readers with sufficient information to satisfy their immediate needs and to serve as an adequate base for further investigation and for asking intelligent questions of health care providers.

—David J. Triggle, Ph.D.
University Professor
School of Pharmacy and Pharmaceutical Sciences
State University of New York at Buffalo

1
Introduction: Steroids and Other Performance-Enhancing Drugs

As a result of 20 years of steroid use, I walk with a limp, I have seven scars on my face, two destroyed knees, and I can't walk up a flight of stairs until I chug a couple cups of black coffee and a handful of anti-inflammatory pills. What strapping 18-year-old athlete could ever imagine ending up with a herniated back disk and a neck that pops like fireworks on the Fourth of July from a mere turn of my head? And those are the obvious problems. The real prizes are a pair of shrunken testicles and surgical scars across my nipples from having breast tissue removed from my chest.

– Dan Clark, a.k.a. Nitro from American Gladiator[1]

In 1982, 18-year-old Dan Clark was a football player looking for a competitive edge after an injury set him back. He knew a guy named Joe from the gym who was huge, ripped, and was what Dan aspired to look like. Joe told Dan that his secret to getting big was steroids.

In the 1980s, there was little outreach and education about the negative impacts of steroids to improve physical performance, so Dan had no apprehensions. With the $125 that his father gave him as a birthday gift, Dan went to Joe's doctor to get his first injection of steroids.

Dan was told by his doctor that steroids are the synthetic version of testosterone—the hormone that makes a man a man. The doctor claimed that Dan would increase his size, strength, and muscle mass, and would be an animal on the football field. That day, Dan received an injectable steroid called testosterone cypionate and an oral steroid called Dianabol (methandrostenolone), commonly called D-bol. Dan was warned of the possible side effects, such as development of breast tissue, but he was assured these effects were rare and that there was another drug he could take to counteract them.

Dan went home with his steroids and was directed to take one Dianabol in the morning and one in the evening. After two weeks, he could increase the dosage to three D-bols a day and, if necessary, four a day if he felt like he was not getting the desired muscle gains. Dan received his first injection of testosterone cypionate in the office with instructions to either inject himself or have a friend inject further doses into the butt cheek, past the layer of fat and into the muscle.

Dan was amazed at how quickly his body responded to the steroids. One day he was benching 185 pounds and the next, he was lifting 225 pounds. He recalls being quicker, stronger, and explosive on the field. Dan also noticed a considerable change in himself psychologically. Gone was his self-doubt, replaced with over-the-top aggression and the belief that he was the best on the field. As with many steroid users, the initial use seemed to only bring good things, like a honeymoon. Unfortunately for Dan, his initial steroid use progressed to abuse and addiction that caused permanent damage to his body and destroyed his personal relationships. Dan now speaks out about the dangers of steroid use.

Steroids are a class of drugs that include the sex hormone **testosterone**. Steroids are classified by their molecular structure, which consists of 17 carbon atoms arranged in four rings. Understanding this molecular structure and tinkering with it has led to the creation of hundreds of synthetic steroids.

Men and women both produce testosterone, although men have approximately 10 times more testosterone than women. Adding testosterone to a woman's body will have a greater biological effect than adding the same amount of testosterone to a man. Steroid use in women tends to have a more masculinizing effect than in men.

Each person has varying levels of testosterone, but in general, men produce about 4 to 7 milligrams of testosterone a day.[2] In men, testosterone is primarily produced in the testicles. In women, it is produced in the ovaries along with the female sex hormone, **estrogen**. A small amount of testosterone is produced in the **adrenal glands**, which produces other hormones, mostly stress-related, and sits above the kidneys.

In men, testosterone levels fluctuate during life, with levels increasing at puberty, peaking in the twenties and decreasing gradually and continuously at age 40 and beyond. As a hormone, testosterone levels change slightly even throughout the day, with generally higher levels in the morning for younger men. Many factors other than age can affect testosterone levels. Husbands generally have lower testosterone than single men, and playing competitive sports also increases testosterone levels. Holding a baby decreases testosterone.

Testosterone is responsible for building muscle, which is referred to as an **anabolic** effect. Testosterone also has an **androgenic** effect, which means it enhances masculine features such as deepening of the voice, increased oil production, increased hair growth, and increased sex drive. In women, this androgenic effect is particularly unwanted, as it leads to the development of facial hair that requires shaving, a deeper voice, and growth of the clitoris.

Steroids are essentially a synthetic version of testosterone or an altered form of testosterone. These synthetic drugs mimic testosterone's anabolic effects and ideally omit the androgenic effect. Most users want the muscle-building qualities of steroids but do not want the **acne** and hair growth from the androgenic aspect of steroids. Despite all the tweaking of modern science, a steroid with only anabolic properties has yet to be developed. To the dismay of many users, all steroids used to enhance performance have some androgenic effect. For this reason, steroids synthesized from testosterone are referred to as **androgenic anabolic steroids (AAS)**. In many cases, steroids are simply referred to as anabolic steroids, but this is not an indication that there is no androgenic effect.

Although some athletes take testosterone to enhance performance, most users take a synthetic form of steroids. For the purposes of this book, steroids will refer to AAS and are defined as any drug or substance chemically and pharmacologically related to testosterone for the purposes of building muscle. In this book, steroids will not include estrogen or **corticosteroids**, since they do not help build muscle. Corticosteroids are commonly used in medicine to treat diseases associated with inflammation such as arthritis or ulcerative colitis.

Although there are hundreds of steroids and other **performance-enhancing drugs (PEDs)** available, this book will cover the most popular ones, including

Deca-Durabolin and Durabolin (nandrolone), Equipoise (boldenone unde-clynate), Sustanon (testosterone blend), Anadrol (oxymetholone), and Winstrol (stanozolol). The common street names for anabolic steroids include Arnolds, gym candy, pumpers, 'roids, stackers, weight trainers, gear, and juice.

Performance-enhancing drugs are compounds that increase athletic performance either due to increased stamina or through an anabolic effect. Steroids are a PED; however, not all PEDs have the chemical structure of steroids, and therefore not all PEDs are steroids. **Erythropoietin** (EPO) is one kind of PED that is not a steroid and does not have an anabolic effect. Darbepoetin is a synthetic form of erythropoietin. It is a hormone that promotes the production of **red blood cells**. Red blood cells deliver oxygen to the body. By having more red blood cells in the body, a person generally has more access to oxygen. This increase in available oxygen offers the athlete more stamina in heavy oxygen-demanding activities such as sprinting on a bicycle.

An increase in red blood cells, however, is not without its dangers. A higher amount of red blood cells makes the blood more thick. Thicker blood increases the possibility of blood clots, heart attacks, strokes, and sudden death. The distinction made between steroids and nonsteroid PEDs does not mean that other PEDs are any less potent than steroids in terms of effect on the body.

THE INTERPLAY OF MUSCLES, PROTEIN, AND STEROIDS

The human body consists of more than 600 muscles made up of elastic tissue. Some of the muscles of the body are considered involuntary, such as the blood-pumping muscles surrounding the heart. Many other muscles are controlled voluntarily, such as the muscles in the arm when a person decides to lift a weight. These muscles are referred to as the **skeletal muscles** and are what people typically think of when they think of increasing muscle size.[3]

The size of muscles can be increased based on diet and exercise alone. Protein is necessary for muscles to grow. Without sufficient protein intake, skeletal muscle will not increase when combined with strength training. Protein requirements depend on age, gender, and weight, but in general men need approximately 56 grams of protein daily and women need 46 grams.

Strength training is a critical aspect of building muscles. Lifting weights is probably what most people perceive as strength training, but other forms of exercise such as yoga offer strength training by using postures to develop muscles. Repeatedly stimulating the muscles through strength training leads to an increase in muscle size, although the mechanism is not well understood. It is known that the response occurs at the cellular level of the muscle, just as it does with steroids.

Steroids increase the size of muscles and shorten the time it takes for muscle mass to increase. In recent years, scientists have discovered that steroids also increase the number of skeletal muscle cells.[4]

Once a steroid molecule has entered the body, it interacts with the skeletal muscle cell. Within each skeletal muscle cell is a **receptor**. Once the steroid molecule enters the receptor, it is able to make changes to the cell; specifically, the steroid molecule increases protein synthesis within the skeletal muscle cell. By increasing protein synthesis within the muscle cell, the muscle grows

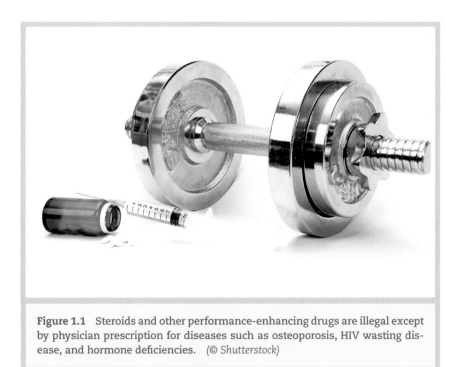

Figure 1.1 Steroids and other performance-enhancing drugs are illegal except by physician prescription for diseases such as osteoporosis, HIV wasting disease, and hormone deficiencies. (© *Shutterstock*)

in size. This process is true whether the steroid is produced naturally in the body, injected, or taken orally.

For optimal muscle building, the three necessary ingredients are anabolic steroids, overloading of skeletal muscle through strength training, and dietary intake of protein above the normal daily requirements.[5] Specifically, it takes about eight to 10 months for a healthy male to add an additional 10 pounds of muscle mass by combining two to three times the daily recommended amount of protein as well as incorporating a strength training program. When a moderate amount of anabolic steroids is added—where *moderate* is defined as two to three times the recommended clinical dose—a healthy man can add this same 10 pounds of muscle with the same diet and exercise routine six to eight months sooner, in just two months.

The value of strength training goes beyond just looking good. A stronger skeletal muscle system helps prevent falls in the elderly and boosts metabolism. Muscles provide the body with strength, balance, and movement, and a stronger skeletal muscle system helps prevent **osteoporosis**. Osteoporosis is the thinning of bone tissue and loss of bone density, which results in bones becoming more brittle and susceptible to breaking.

Strength training helps prevent osteoporosis. Strength training includes weight training, either with freestanding weights or weighted machines, as well as resistance training, which uses equipment such as elastic bands to build muscle. Strength training also increases bone density and helps prevent osteoporosis. In addition, steroids increase bone mineral density and bone strength, especially when combined with resistance training. However, all the evidence of an increase in bone mineral density from the use of artificial steroids has been with people who have osteoporosis. There is no scientific evidence that bone mineral density would increase in healthy individuals. Adding muscle mass to the body will also help boost a person's metabolism, since muscle burns calories but fat does not. Strong abdominal muscles help maintain support in the body, taking pressure and usually pain off the back.

THE PROS AND CONS OF STEROIDS AND OTHER PERFORMANCE-ENHANCING DRUGS

Steroids and other PEDs offer many benefits in addition to an increase in muscle mass and strength. These drugs can enhance blood volume and hemoglobin concentrations, decrease body fat, reduce reflex time, increase mental intensity, increase pain tolerance, and as mentioned above, increase bone density in those who are suffering from osteoporosis. Not all steroids and PEDs offer these benefits, however, and achieving the right dose is critical.

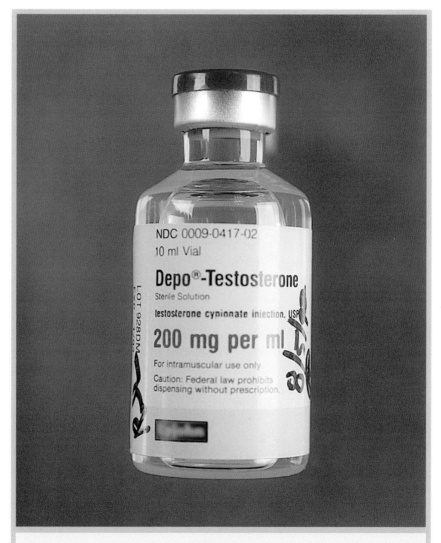

Figure 1.2 Lab-synthesized testosterone, which has valid medical uses, is sometimes diverted and used illegally. Testosterone is responsible for building muscle and has an androgenic, or masculinizing, effect. (© *Drug Enforcement Administration*)

Cancer and AIDS Patients

Steroids are approved by the U.S. Food and Drug Administration (FDA) for people who are suffering from a muscle-wasting disease such as acquired immunodeficiency syndrome (AIDS) or cancer. Individuals in this situation benefit from steroids because they generally experience an increase in muscle mass and report an increase in appetite, increased well-being, and reduced weakness.

SHOULD WE ALLOW STEROIDS AND OTHER PEDS IN SPORTS?

Taking drugs to enhance athletic performance is considered cheating by most people because it creates unnatural advantages. Athletes who choose to abide by the rules and not take steroids or PEDs are put at a disadvantage if other athletes are taking drugs. In 2003, elite track coach Trevor Graham obtained a sample of an anabolic steroid (AAS) called the "Clear," and gave it to the US Anti-Doping Agency to add to the chain of steroid tests. The drug had not yet been added to the list of drugs tested for by Graham at that time, however. Graham knew about the Clear and felt it was unfair that users were taking it and not getting caught simply because the Anti-Doping Agency was not aware of it. The Anti-Doping Agency added the Clear to its list of drugs for which it tests. Eventually, athletes who used this drug were caught by the Anti-Doping Agency. Most people hold the same opinion as Graham—that taking PEDs is cheating. There are those individuals, however, who disagree.

   An opposing viewpoint suggests that taking PEDs to compete better is no different than taking FDA-approved drugs to offer the average person an enhanced lifestyle. People with attention-deficit/hyperactivity disorder (ADHD) often take a drug such as Ritalin or Adderall so that they can perform better. Individuals who are

nervous about

Primary Hypogonadism and Other Hormone-Related Disorders

Steroids and **human growth hormone** (HGH) can be life-changing for individuals suffering from a disorder wherein the body is not producing the sufficient amount of hormones. One condition is **primary hypogonadism**, a condition in which the testes produce little or no hormones. By supplementing

public speaking might choose to take a beta-blocker or an antianxiety drug such as Xanax. Tony Newman, director of media relations at the Drug Policy Alliance, asks, "Who among us isn't enhancing their performance?" Newman believes that we should never incarcerate someone for putting a substance into his or her body if no harm is done to anyone else.[6]

Although it is true that drugs such as Adderall are taken to enhance performance, it is not quite comparable to a bicyclist taking erythropoietin (EPO) or a bodybuilder taking **trenbolone** ("Tren"). Adderall is a drug that underwent extensive research before it was approved by the FDA and brought to the marketplace. Many of the steroids and PEDs have no FDA-approved human use, so their safety is unknown. In addition, people who take drugs such as Adderall are under the care of a physician, who monitors their health while they are taking this drug.

Requiring a prescription is one way to help prevent abuse of the drug. People taking steroids and other PEDs are usually purchasing their drugs on the black market, taking doses much higher than what would be recommended, and staying on these drugs for a longer period than has ever been studied. The main difference between the illegal and medically unsupervised use of steroids and other PEDs and the use of FDA-approved drugs that enhance the quality of life is that the illegal use of drugs puts the user's health in danger.

with a steroid, a boy with this condition can reach puberty and achieve all the male sexual characteristics that a male without the disorder would.

Steroids can also be to treat sexual dysfunction in postmenopausal women. Menopause is tremendously disruptive to a woman's hormones, and many women suffer from lack of sex drive. Steroids have been shown to help correct this imbalance.

HGH is used for several growth hormone-related disorders such as growth hormone deficiency. HGH can also be used in children with short stature that is not caused by a medical condition to achieve an extra two or three inches in height.

THE ABUSE OF STEROIDS

Steroids are used for medicinal purposes, but are often abused to improve athletic performance or appearance. The abuse of steroids follows a similar pattern of drug addiction, where those that are addicted will continue to use steroids even after recognizing that the drug is damaging their body and relationships. In an experiment at Harvard University, hamsters self-administered steroids to the point of death.[7]

A unique characteristic of steroid addiction is that, unlike other drugs of abuse such as cocaine, heroin, or nicotine, steroids are not believed to induce an immediate intoxicating or rewarding effect. The changes in the body take time.

The administration of steroids and other PEDs by trainers and athletes is referred to as **doping**. Doping can take many forms: tablets, injections, and even withdrawing and reinjecting one's own blood. Although steroid possession and use without a prescription is illegal, proving that an athlete has been doping can be extremely difficult.

PREVALENCE OF STEROID USE

The National Institute on Drug Abuse (NIDA) estimates that more than 500,000 eighth through 10th grade students are now using steroids, and increasing numbers of high school seniors do not believe steroids are risky. In another survey, by the International Survey Associates, in Bowling Green,

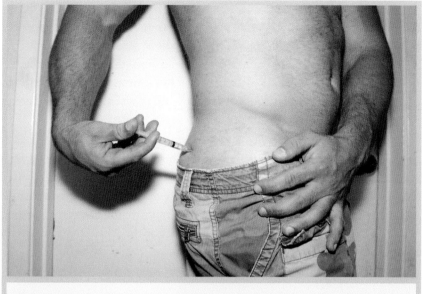

Figure 1.3 Steroids are most often administered by injection into muscle.
(© *Newscom*)

Kentucky, 2 percent of junior high students reported using steroids in the past year, and almost 5 percent of 12th graders reported steroid use.[8]

Steroid use is also higher in boys than in girls, with an estimated 7.1 percent of 12th grade males reporting steroid use as compared with 2.7 percent of 12th grade females.[9] Whereas steroids were primarily used by athletes in the early days of their discovery, the scope of people using steroids and other PEDs to enhance their performance and image has grown to include many professions and a wide span of ages.

HUMAN GROWTH HORMONE

Human growth hormone (HGH) is a naturally occurring protein-based hormone for growth and metabolism. HGH is produced in the pituitary gland, which is located at the base of the brain. Given HGH's role in growth and development, levels decline around age 20. Many products are sold on the Internet that promote HGH as an antiaging product. These claims have not been supported by any legitimate medical studies.

HGH has been used by competitive athletes since the 1970s to boost performance, since HGH is believed to have anabolic properties. In addition to increasing muscle mass, HGH is believed by many users of the drug to reduce body fat and support a "ripped" physique.

Because HGH occurs naturally in the body, it was nearly impossible to detect synthetic HGH in blood tests, which increased its popularity with competing athletes. As with many PEDs, the popularity of the drug is often linked to how easy it is to take it without detection. In 2004, however, anti-doping professionals enhanced blood tests to improve the chances of finding HGH users, and employed the new techniques at the 2004 Olympic Games in Athens.

2
Historical Use of Steroids and Other Performance-Enhancing Drugs

In January 1986, Dan Duchaine was eating lunch in an Italian restaurant with two friends in Carlsbad, California, hatching a plan to make a ton of money. One of his friends was 34-year-old David Jenkins, a former Olympic track medalist, and the other friend was William Dillon, a former bodybuilder who held the Mr. Collegiate Illinois title while he attended Southern Illinois University. All three men had experience with steroids, and over lunch they planned to get wealthy from the public's demand to look or compete better.

Duchaine's experience was as a wholesaler who made steroids out of his own home. Jenkins had taken steroids to be more competitive in the Olympics, and Dillon had started taking steroids and then began selling steroids to support his habit. Duchaine proposed that the three of them work together to manufacture Dianabol in Mexico for sale in the United States. Dillon was a businessman and Duchaine had great contacts in the drug world. Together they felt they were destined for success. In addition, anabolic steroid laws at that time were fairly weak. The men perceived that any potential legal penalty was worth the financial gain. Duchaine reminded his two friends that another steroid dealer, Tony Fitton, who had been described as the largest steroid dealer in the world when he was arrested in 1984, would likely serve less than a year in jail.

The three men decided their first task was to get a supplier in Mexico. In February 1986, Jenkins flew to Tijuana, and went to the doorstep of Laboratorios Milanos to speak to the president, Juan Macklis. Macklis owned a drug factory that was so well protected from intruders that there were armed guards standing outside. Macklis was believed to be well connected, particularly with corrupt police officers who helped hide his operations.

Jenkins asked Macklis what he would charge to manufacture 100 tablets of Dianabol. Even with Macklis's markup, Jenkins realized he could make a considerable profit. Within three months, Macklis had manufactured $30,000 worth of steroids, and Jenkins filled suitcases with the bottles to give to Dillon and Duchaine. To make it appear that the steroids were of high quality, the three created counterfeit European pharmaceutical labels for the bottles.

Their operation continued to grow as the three indulged in a lavish lifestyle that included $1,000 bottles of wine, a Maserati, and heavy partying. With the extravagant lifestyle that they were living, they eventually attracted the attention of the federal government. The Los Angeles Police Department eventually raided Dillon's home and found the fake steroid labels. Although Dillon knew it was not illegal to possess such labels, he was uncomfortable living with the police watching him and got out of the illegal steroid business. Duchaine had little fear as he continued selling steroids, becoming known as a steroid guru and the author of the notorious Underground Steroid Handbook. *Duchaine eventually served two federal prison sentences for drug dealing.*

Duchaine, Jenkins, and Dillon are just a few of the many players in the world of steroid sellers. The 1980s was a time when many of the influential people in the business of manufacturing and distribution of steroids got their start.

THE HISTORY OF TESTOSTERONE

In 1926, a young University of Chicago medical student named Lemuel C. McGee, along with his professor, Dr. Frederick Koch, acquired 40 pounds of bull testicles to experiment with. At this time, testosterone had not yet been isolated. From the bull testicles, the pair were able to extract 20 milligrams of what they believed to be the male sex hormone testosterone.

To prove their **hypothesis**, they used an old experiment where the hormone is injected into a neutered rooster, also called a **capon**. A capon's behavior is different than that of a rooster due to its lack of sex hormones. A capon is generally more docile and less prone to fighting, in addition to lacking sexual instincts. The lack of testosterone also causes physical changes in a capon such as a lack of comb and wattles, which are the red appendages around the rooster's face.

Within two weeks of being injected with testosterone, the animal began to behave and look like a rooster. Like all good researchers, McGee and Koch decided to perform their experiment again to see if they would get the same results. They did. The two scientists felt certain that they had proven the discovery of testosterone, which scientists had been in search of for two centuries.

The next step was to perform experiments on humans, specifically a male lacking testosterone such as a **eunuch**. A eunuch is a castrated man, often castrated prior to puberty to serve as singers, servants, and guardians of women, primarily in ancient Greece and Rome. Koch and McGee, along with another scientist, Dr. Charles Kenyon, were not surprised that their injection also produced masculinizing traits in the eunuch.

Although the three scientists knew where the male hormone came from, they still needed to isolate it completely in the hopes of recreating it in a lab, a process known as synthesis. In 1935, a German pharmacologist named Ernest Lacquer from Amsterdam was able to extract pure testosterone and determine its exact molecular structure. Determining the molecular structure of the compound is essential to recreating the compound.

Before Lacquer, the male sex hormone did not have a name. The name *testosterone* is credited to Lacquer. While Lacquer was creating testosterone, Leopold Ružička, a chemist from Yugoslavia, and Adolf Butendant, a German chemist, were able to synthesize the hormone from cholesterol.[1] Once testosterone was isolated and could be synthesized, it was made available to the medical community for the treatment of disease.

Testosterone, despite its beneficial uses, was first used as a drug of abuse. The Nazi Party had been in power for a couple of years during the time of testosterone's synthesis and they began to use it on their Olympic athletes. In many cases, these athletes took testosterone unknowingly or against their will.

ATHLETES AND STEROIDS IN THE 1960s

One of the first steroids to become popular in the 1960s was **methandros-tenolone**, brand name *Dianabol*, often referred to as "D-bol." Dianabol was created and marketed by Ciba Pharmaceuticals in 1958. Dianabol was preferred to testosterone due to its fewer side effects. Once Dianabol become popular, many athletes switched to Dianabol from testosterone.

Dr. John Ziegler, a U.S. weight-lifting team's doctor, switched the U.S. team over from testosterone to Dianabol in 1958 when it became available to avoid the masculinizing effects of testosterone. At the time, Dr. Ziegler was not doing anything illegal. Dr. Ziegler experimented on the weight lifters with Dianabol in different doses and published his findings in fitness journals. Dr. Ziegler's findings contributed to the widespread popularity of Dianabol.

In 1960, the use of PEDs was not prohibited during Olympic competition. Before the decade was out, however, the International Olympic Committee would implement its first rules against doping, and the first athlete to test positive for a banned substance had to give up his medal.[2]

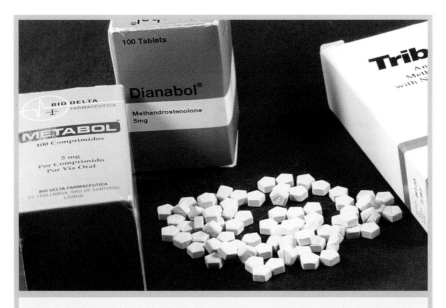

Figure 2.1 Dianabol, an early steroid first manufactured in 1958, became popular in the 1960s, as it produced fewer side effects than lab-synthesized testosterone. *(© Alamy)*

Dianabol also became popular with football players in the 1960s. Dianabol was reportedly placed in cereal bowls on the training table of the 1963 San Diego Chargers by their coach, Alvin Roy. Roy learned about Dianabol from Ziegler. The 1960s were just the beginning of Dianabol's word-of-mouth popularity by athletes.

STEROIDS IN THE 1970s

During the 1970s, East Germany was a country well known for requiring its Olympic athletes to take steroids. Due to the political climate in East Germany, many athletes were not given a choice and some were unknowingly doped. Potential gold medal winners were recruited early on and trained by coaches who received incentives if their athlete won a medal, strongly encouraging the use of steroids. The system to win gold medals in East Germany was named "sports theme plan 1425" and created in 1974 in preparation of the 1976 Olympics in Montreal. The East German team won 40 gold medals, and its female swimmers in particular were dominant, winning 11 of 13 events.[3]

East German sport scientists created a new anabolic steroid called **Oral-Turinabol**.[4] Although steroid use in the Olympics was banned even then, the coaches knew how to mask detection by administering just the right dose.

In 1976, athletes from East Germany were the first to introduce steroids to women's swimming. In Steven Ungerleider's book *Faust's Gold*, American athletes commented on the unfairness of East Germany's steroid advantage and what they perceived as the disturbing behavior and appearance of these women. One American Olympic swimmer said, "We would be in the locker room with these female swimmers and we would have to check the symbol on the door to make sure we had the right bathrooms. These swimmers had shoulders like Dallas Cowboys, hair growing all over their bodies." In addition to the masculine features of these women, their attitudes were also very different. "They would spit on the floor. They would look at you like they wanted to rip your tongue out."[5] One result of East Germany's doping agenda is that more athletes from other countries felt like they had to take steroids to have any chance of winning, particularly in women's swimming.

American athletes, in the Olympics and in professional sports, were also being encouraged to take steroids, and there was considerable pressure to take these drugs to win. Steroids were making their way into professional football, with more teams accused of pumping up their athletes than others.

Figure 2.2 The East German 1976 Olympic women's swimming team was given performance-enhancing drugs in an effort to win more medals. (© *Getty Images*)

The Pittsburgh Steelers were a team rumored for their use of steroids.[6] In his 1990 book, *God's Coach*, Skip Bayless tells the story of Randy White, a Dallas Cowboys player who used steroids during the 1970s, claiming that he felt intimidated by the Steelers' linemen.

STEROIDS IN THE 1980s: THE EMERGENCE OF EPO AND HGH

By the 1980s, steroids and other PEDs were widely used, but athletes were getting caught, which ruined their endorsement deals and careers. For this reason, many athletes turned to human growth hormone (HGH) and erythropoietin (EPO). Although anti-doping professionals were aware of these drugs, a test had not been developed to prove that an athlete had taken EPO or HGH.

EPO is a natural hormone produced by the kidneys that boosts red blood cell production. EPO had legitimate uses in the marketplace for people who

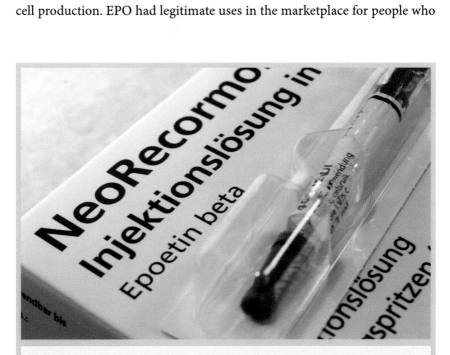

Figure 2.3   Erythropoietin (EPO) is a natural hormone produced by the kidneys that increases red blood cell production. Synthetic EPO, shown, is used illegally as a performance-enhancing drug.   (© *AP Images*)

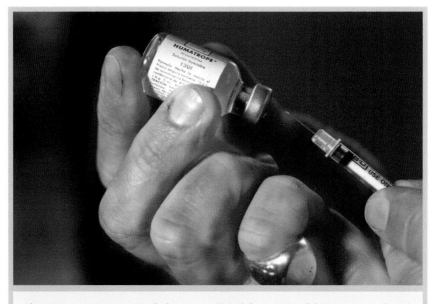

Figure 2.4 Human growth hormone (HGH) is a natural hormone produced by the pituitary gland. Synthetic HGH, shown, is abused as a performance-enhancing drug. *(© Alamy)*

suffered from diseases that caused a deficiency in red cell production, such as anemia. The 1980s brought new techniques to mass-produce this natural hormone. Clinical trials of EPO began in Europe and by 1989, EPO-related drugs were approved by the FDA. Although clinical trials are meant to bring drugs to the market to cure legitimate ailments, the process also makes these drugs more available for illicit purposes. The combination of new methods of EPO production and the lack of adequate testing to detect EPO led to its popularity by endurance athletes such as bicyclists.

During the 1980s, a company named Genentech was the first to develop a synthetic form of HGH to treat individuals who had naturally low levels of the hormone. Prior to the creation of a synthetic version of HGH, a limited supply of HGH was available from the pituitary glands of cadavers. Once a synthetic version was developed, the supply of HGH, and therefore the potential for its abuse, increased. HGH's reputation as a wonder drug spread quickly among athletes and bodybuilders, even though at the time it was considered a costly drug, with some athletes reportedly paying $500 per week.

THE HISTORY OF DRUG TESTING

When it comes to testing for steroids, not all sports are treated equally. Athletes in the Olympics are more highly scrutinized than baseball players. In the 1988 Olympic Games, Canadian Ben Johnson set a world record for the 100-meter dash: 9.79 seconds. But Johnson tested positive for the steroid stanozolol and the gold medal was awarded to Carl Lewis, who came in second.

Baseball is the sport that many anti-doping experts have argued has been the most lax in testing its athletes, with testing beginning in 2003. Prior to that, most players doped freely, causing the years between 1992 and 2001 to be dubbed the "steroid era" by many.

In 2008, baseball boasted a mere three players who tested positive, but many people argue that athletes have found ways to avoid testing positive. Often the date of steroid testing is announced well in advance, which enables the user to stop taking steroids long enough for it to clear out of the body. The user then resumes taking the drug after the test has been completed.

The success of Alex Rodriguez, known as A-Rod, is one example of the ineffective anti-doping program in baseball. Rodriguez is regarded as one of the best baseball players of all time and was the youngest player ever to hit 600 home runs. Rodriguez never tested positive for steroids or PEDs but admitted in February 2009 to having used steroids from 2001 to 2003. In 2007, A-Rod had denied using PEDs, even in a TV interview on *60 Minutes* with Katie Couric.

The element of surprise is a crucial part of any successful drug testing program. If a person is given enough notice about a drug test, he or she can usually avoid getting caught. Steroid and other PED testing has progressed considerably today; if an athlete has used a banned drug and has not had time to stop use before being tested, he or she will likely be caught.

STEROIDS AND THE BLACK MARKET

The distribution of steroids by people seeking to enhance their athletic performance or appearance has changed dramatically since steroids were banned.

WHAT IS BLOOD DOPING?

Blood doping is a practice of competitive athletes where the person withdraws blood, usually a pint, and then stores it in a bag for approximately three to six weeks. During the period when the blood is stored, the athlete's body will replenish this missing blood. Timing is critical in blood doping to ensure that the person's body has replenished the missing blood supply. If the time frame is too short to allow the body to compensate for the missing blood, then the advantage of blood doping is lost. Immediately prior to a competition, the athlete will transfuse the blood back into the body, thus providing extra blood, therefore extra red blood cells and a boost in stamina. This process is often referred to as **autotransfusion**.

Blood doping has been a popular practice of endurance athletes since the early 1980s. By 1986, it was banned from competition, although it would be many years more before a test could be developed to reliably detect the practice.

Similar to many illegal drugs, steroids are sold through a hushed, "word-of-mouth" network of dealers, who usually are users themselves. Selling steroids often helps to financially support their expensive habit. Bodybuilding shows and gyms are two common places where users purchase steroids.

The unsanitary and unregulated conditions of illegal steroid manufacturing is a significant concern. In one federal enforcement action, named Operation Raw Deal, officials raided labs that revealed large amounts of raw materials being mixed in bathtubs and bathroom sinks. Unlike steroids sold for legitimate reasons through legal channels, illegal steroids do not pass the scrutiny of the FDA, nor do manufacturers institute any quality controls to ensure that their products are safe. Taking an illegal drug is risky because there is no way of knowing what the drug is or if it was prepared properly. When people buy steroids on the black market, they are giving up

Blood doping was banned because it offers an unfair advantage just as drugs do, but also because it is highly dangerous. By adding red blood cells to the body unnaturally, the blood becomes thicker and therefore more likely to clog capillaries. This situation causes an increased chance of blood clots and other blood-related diseases such as stroke (when blood becomes clogged in the brain) and heart attack (when blood becomes clogged in the heart).

Despite the risks and illegal status of blood doping, athletes and their trainers continue to autotranfuse. One of the appeals of blood doping is that it is often harder to detect than drugs are. Attempts have been made to test for blood doping, such as evaluating the number of red blood cells in the body. The results can be highly variable, however, and as with most doping practices, it became easy for athletes to figure out how to make sure they did not exceed the numbers in the test to disqualify themselves. In some cases, athletes or trainers have been caught with bags of blood. Floyd Landis, the 2006 Tour de France winner (later stripped of his title), who admitted to using steroids and PEDs, claimed that he held bags of blood for Lance Armstrong to autotransfuse later.

the protection of organizations that are set up to ensure that the drugs that Americans take are safe.

HISTORY OF BENEFICIAL USES OF STEROIDS AND OTHER PERFORMANCE-ENHANCING DRUGS

When scientists discovered the molecular structure of testosterone, the intent of drug manufacturers and scientists was to further the treatment of disease, not to help athletes compete better. Although the discovery and synthesis of testosterone occurred in the 1920s and 1930s, the manufacture and FDA approval of steroids did not occur until much later.

Steroids such as oxandrolone were created in 1964 to promote muscle growth for people suffering from disorders that caused weight loss and osteoporosis. Stanozolol was created in 1965 to treat osteoporosis, specifically corticosteroid-induced osteoporosis. Steroids and other PEDs such as HGH continue to treat disease and disorders, and the number of disorders treated has increased to include **HIV wasting disease**, muscle loss from cancer, and other ailments.

STEROID AND PED USE TODAY

The type of people using steroids and their purposes in doing so has changed considerably over the past few decades. Steroid use has expanded from professional athletes to those looking to enhance their body image, including junior high school students, police officers, firefighters, fraternity brothers, military personnel, and bodybuilders. Steroids build muscle and reduce fat. For athletes and professional bodybuilders, there is an obvious benefit to taking these drugs. Although the payoff for others is not in the form of winning competitions or earning medals, people, primarily men, may feel a more muscular image is worth the expense and health risk of taking steroids.

Many users report that they like the feeling of looking big and tough, so as to intimidate other men and boost their ego. For other groups, such as fitness buffs and college students, taking steroids to enhance their body is often motivated by a desire to look good to their peers and attract sexual partners.

In the book *Inside Greek U.*, author Alan DeSantis discovers in his interviews with fraternity members that steroids are a growing trend among these men. According to Robert, a fraternity member who was interviewed for the book, Deca (nandrolone) is a common steroid used by members. In addition, due to the stigma of steroids, users generally cover for one another, denying any knowledge of a fraternity brother using steroids. Another fraternity member interviewed said that **creatine** (a legal substance normally found in muscles) is one of the most common products used to get bigger, but he knew other guys in the fraternity house that used other supplements containing **ephedra**.[7]

3

Biological Mechanisms of Steroids and Other Performance-Enhancing Drugs

Dan thought Angie was beautiful and charming. A former bodybuilder, she had cinnamon-brown eyes and an amazing body. When she was competing, Angie's body was so muscular that she had 16-inch arms. Angie eventually quit bodybuilding and her masculine physique disappeared.

After a few weeks of dating, Angie began to cry and told Dan that she had a secret. Angie told Dan that she used to take steroids, starting on her eighteenth birthday and continuing for another 10 years. Taking steroids consistently and following the bodybuilding circuit made her endure a life of vomiting, urinating blood, getting into street fights, and getting arrested. The steroids stripped away her femininity and she developed acne and facial hair that turned to whiskers. It seemed normal when she had to shave her face because all the other female bodybuilders were doing it. Eventually she suffered considerable hair loss and she resembled a cancer patient. Dan was a user of steroids, so he was familiar with the side effects she described, until she showed him the one he had never seen before: an enlarged clitoris. Angie told him that she took a lot of testosterone and it caused her clitoris to grow.

Angie used estrogen therapy to regain some of her femininity. In addition to the enlarged clitoris, Angie was also left sterile. Angie admitted that the sight of babies made her deeply depressed.[1]

INTRODUCTION: BIOLOGICAL EFFECTS OF STEROIDS

Steroids are taken to alter the skeletal muscle system. In the human body, all systems are integrated and altering one will inevitably have an effect on the others, such as the reproductive system or circulatory system. The extent of this effect depends on a person's own chemistry, the drug taken, its dosage, the duration of use, and the presence of other medications in the person's system.

Two steroids can have very similar molecular structures and still cause quite different reactions. In the creation of different steroids, scientists alter the molecular structure of testosterone yet still maintain the basic structure of a steroid: the specific four rings. In general, steroids have been altered to maximize the anabolic effect and minimize the androgenic or masculinizing effect.

The scientific literature is limited on the use of steroids and other PEDs for the purposes of athletic performance, particularly for long-term use (a decade or more). The short-term effects of steroids and other PEDs are much better documented and understood by the medical community, even use by healthy adults. The legal uses of steroids are for people with actual medical problems such as a muscle wasting disease, and the manner in which steroids are used to cure medical conditions is different from how athletes use the drug. One important difference is the dosage. Often the dosage taken by athletes is two or three times higher than the recommended dose for medicinal use. In the case of designer drugs or other steroids that do not have an approved use for human consumption, there is no recommended dosage, so any dosage is a guess at safety.

The other critical factor in evaluating the biological implications of taking steroids is the common practice of **stacking**, where users take steroids together. Combining drugs presents a danger, as a drug might behave differently in the body in the presence of another drug. Most steroid users take more than one steroid simultaneously; in addition, they might be taking other supplements, too. Predicting how a steroid will react in a person's body becomes increasingly complex when drugs are combined. Athletes, bodybuilders, and others seeking the perfect physique are performing self-experimentation and willingly share the results on Internet bodybuilding message boards. This

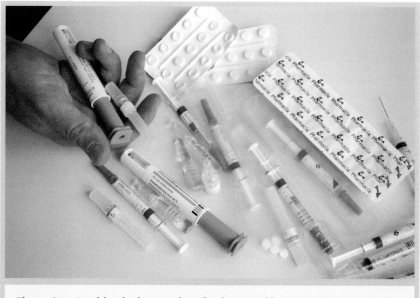

Figure 3.1 Stacking is the practice of using steroids or PEDs in combination, and presents additional dangers to the user's health. *(© Corbis)*

chapter will explore the scientific research that is available on how these drugs work, but also the reported results from users who abuse steroids.

HOW STEROIDS ENHANCE PROTEIN SYNTHESIS

Protein is necessary to build muscles. Steroids enhance protein synthesis in the body. Steroid molecules do this by entering the muscle cell, which not all molecules can do. When the steroid molecule enters the cell, it binds to a receptor within the cell known as the steroid-receptor complex. The binding of steroid to this receptor in the muscle leads to a change in gene expression or "behavior" of the cell within hours or days. Interestingly, strength training also alters gene expression.

This change in gene expression is a pivotal part of how the cells within the muscle increase. A change in gene expression leads to an increase in cell size through protein synthesis. An increase in skeletal muscle cells leads to an increase in muscle size.

STEROID REGIMES

The steroid regime that a person follows greatly affects the biological effect of the drug. A woman taking steroids to treat osteoporosis at the recommended dose is less likely to experience hair growth on her face and acne on her back than a female bodybuilder taking steroids to build muscle. A bodybuilder taking three times the dose of the woman with osteoporosis and combining that drug with another anabolic steroid is more likely to experience unwanted side effects. Therefore, presenting the manner in which steroids are often taken is crucial to understanding the biological mechanisms of these drugs.

STEROID CYCLES

A **steroid cycle** is the number of days the user chooses to take the drug continuously before stopping use. Many users feel that by "cycling" steroid use, they will give their body a break and allow it to begin producing its own testosterone again. Shrunken testicles are the result of the body no longer producing much, if any, testosterone because the user is essentially injecting testosterone. The body is efficient: if testosterone is being injected, the body will cease production and then the testicles will shrivel up.

Many steroid users believe cycling will prevent short- and long-term side effects. Another reason many people cycle their steroids and other PEDs is to minimize cost. Enhancing one's performance or appearance comes at a heavy price, in hundreds to thousands of dollars. Floyd Landis claimed that he spent $90,000 annually on PEDs, although this is likely on the very high side.

Despite the support of steroid cycling in the bodybuilding culture, scientific studies have not been completed to determine what advantages cycling offers. The danger of repeatedly going on and off steroids is that the user will likely experience fatigue, depression, sexual dysfunction, and other symptoms associated with withdrawal when they are "off," causing many users to shorten the rest between cycles. To prevent the intense feelings of withdrawal, some users choose to stay on a low dose of steroids or other PEDs continuously and cycle higher doses.

Designing a Cycle

After deciding to take steroids for the first time, most users will "design" their first cycle based on talking to other steroid users, usually from the individual's gym or athletic team, as well as using information available on Internet bodybuilding forums.

Many beginners will take one steroid in their first cycle to see how that one particular drug affects their body. By introducing one steroid at a time, the user will be able to discern the benefits and unwanted side effects that are specific to his body chemistry. Users often take notes on the gains they experience, as well as any side effects. Most users recognize that everyone's body is different. In addition, the goals that a user has will affect his or her choice of steroids.

Cutting Versus Bulking

From the perspective of an athlete or bodybuilder designing a cycle, steroids are divided into two distinct categories. The first category is steroids that aid "cutting." In bodybuilding, a "cut" body is one that has very little body fat and has well-defined muscles. Stanozolol (Winstrol) and oxandrolone (Anavar) are known as the best cutting steroids. They are all derived from the hormone dihydrotestosterone (DHT). DHT is chemically very similar to testosterone and is produced naturally in the body. The production of DHT is linked to baldness.

One of the most endearing aspects of DHT from the perspective of bodybuilders and athletes is that, unlike some steroids, DHT does not convert to estrogen in the body. By avoiding inadvertent adding of estrogen to the body by taking steroids, users experience less water and fat retention and less breast tissue development than with steroids that can convert to estrogen in the body. Bodybuilders sometimes refer to the steroids that do not convert to estrogen in the body as antiestrogens.

"Bulking," in bodybuilding, refers to increasing size with the desire to gain weight as quickly as possible. By bulking up, a man will look quite large even underneath his clothes, and many steroid users report liking the notion of walking into a room and being the hugest guy there. The steroids best known for bulking are testosterone are D-bol, Deca-Durabolin, and Anadrol. Individuals who choose bulking steroids might start off with one steroid but typically will move to combining a couple of bulking steroids. The unwanted side effects of bulking steroids are bloating, fat retention, and possible breast development, since these steroids can convert to estrogen in the body.

Some users will design a cycle from the very beginning that involves taking more than one steroid. Many bodybuilding sites recommend taking testosterone as a base of their cycle. Because steroids inhibit natural testosterone production, adding testosterone to a cycle is thought to prevent side effects. Scientific evidence supporting this hypothesis, however, is not available.

Dosage and Duration

A person taking steroids to enhance physique or performance will likely take a dose anywhere from two to five times the clinically recommended dose, assuming the drug even has a legitimate medical use, and will continue for a cycle of six to twelve weeks. In a 2008 survey of 37 steroid users, all the men interviewed said their cycle lasted for 12 weeks.[2] Another reason why users cycle is to reduce the high cost of steroid use. Floyd Landis claimed that he spent $90,000 a year using steroids, EPO, and human growth hormone. For nonprofessional athletes who do not make money from enhancing their athletic performance, the expense often limits the duration or dose. Even for those individuals who take these drugs recreationally, it is easy to spend hundreds or thousands of dollars annually just for the sake of looking huge or ripped.

For individuals who want to bulk up quickly, the doses of steroids they take are often more than five times the recommended clinical dose. This dosage is enough to see gains of up to 10 pounds of muscle in just two months.

In general, steroid users during their first cycle will experience a boost of self-esteem, energy, and sex drive. Those just beginning steroid use are generally more wary of preventing damage to their bodies, and will therefore restrict their steroid use to one drug, and stop taking the drug once their cycle is up.

After the cycle is finished and the person is no longer taking any steroids or other PEDs, the person will likely experience depression and fatigue. In addition, the person will lose some muscle mass, and usually a measure of self-esteem along with the muscle loss. Although scientific studies, most completed in the 1970s, show that steroids do increase muscle mass and strength in as little as six to eight weeks, there is no scientific evidence that taking a break after a cycle is a safer or more effective way to take steroids.[3]

Despite the lack of scientific evidence, steroid users embrace this notion that "cycling" steroids allows the body to return to normal in terms of producing testosterone and prevents permanent damage. *Permanently* stopping steroids does offer some hope that the biochemical changes that occur during steroid use will return to normal. During steroid use, **blood pressure** usually increases and the liver can suffer as it tries to flush the poison out of the body. In one study, three months after long-term users stopped taking steroids, most had their blood pressure, lipoprotein profiles, and liver enzymes return to normal.[4]

Front-loading

Front-loading is a technique by steroid and other PED users where higher drug doses are taken in the first few days or weeks of use. By taking higher amounts in the beginning, the user believes that performance gains will occur more quickly.

"The poison is in the dose," is an oft-heard motto in medicine, meaning nearly any substance taken in too high a dose can cause adverse side effects or death. Salt in moderation will not harm the body, but if it is taken in large enough doses, it can cause high blood pressure and other ailments. With steroids, front-loading presents an added danger of taking a dose that will have an adverse effect on the body such as damage to the heart, stroke, or liver damage.

Stacking

When two or more steroids or other PEDs are used at the same time, it is called *stacking*. Users stack anabolic steroids with other drugs to help maximize the results of their cycle. Users believe stacking enables them to benefit from the varying effects of each anabolic steroid and is the absolute best way to achieve maximum muscle gains. Often, a person will combine oral steroids with injectables. Many recreational bodybuilders and other nonprofessional athletes list cost as one of the reasons for not stacking. Whereas a 12-week oral cycle averages approximately $300 to $500 and an injectable cycle costs approximately $600 to $800, a stacked cycle costs approximately $1,200 to $1,500.[5]

By taking more than one steroid at a time, the user is at greater risk of suffering from side effects. Within a steroid cycle, the users will often stack other non-anabolic drugs into their program to help minimize these steroid side effects. This strategy may offer nothing more than a false sense of security, which bodybuilding Web sites offer in plenty.

DRUG INTERACTIONS

Another potential danger of PED use is an adverse drug interaction. Even an FDA-approved drug prescribed by a physician may interact negatively with steroids or other PEDs. Some drugs behave differently in the presence of other drugs. If a woman is taking a birth control pill as prescribed, she has approximately a 99 percent chance of preventing pregnancy. If, however, she takes antibiotics, her chances of preventing pregnancy go down considerably. The antibiotic reduces the effectiveness of the birth control pill, and this is considered a drug interaction.

Typically, when a person is prescribed a drug by a physician, the doctor will have a full list of all medications, supplements, and vitamins that the person takes to know if there is a possibility of an adverse drug interaction. In the situation where a woman taking birth control pills is prescribed an antibiotic, many doctors will warn women of this interaction. When people are taking steroids illegally, however, they generally do not have a doctor to warn them of any drug interactions.

One drug interaction associated with anabolic steroids is an increased sensitivity to oral **anticoagulants**. An anticoagulant is a medication that prevents the blood from clotting. One use of an anticoagulant would be to prevent stroke. If a patient needed to take steroids and an anticoagulant, the dosage of the anticoagulant should be decreased and the patient should be closely monitored.

DESIGNER STEROIDS

Designer steroids are synthetic anabolic-androgenic steroids that were created to avoid detection in a drug test. Designer steroids were created by people such as Patrick Arnold with the intent to enhance performance while evading detection. Designer steroids have never been evaluated for safety or effectiveness by the FDA.

The Clear: THG (Tetrahydrogestrinone)

Tim Montgomery has complained all summer about not getting the financial respect from meet promoters he thought was due the world's second-fastest sprinter. He refused to run races at Athens in June and Berlin eight days ago because the appearance fees were too low.

Montgomery changed all that in 9.78 seconds Saturday at the Grand Prix Final in Paris. Not only did his world record for the 100 meters earn him an instant $250,000, it should triple his appearance fee to an estimated $60,000 per meet next season.

—Philip Hersh, *Chicago Tribune*, September 15, 2002[6]

Tim Montgomery had Patrick Arnold to thank for his victory. **Tetrahydro-gestrinone (THG)** is one of the "designer" steroids developed by Patrick Arnold. Arnold used the banned anabolic steroids gestrinone and trenbo-lone as his inspiration when creating THG. In 2001, Arnold ordered raw materials from China and then created THG in his Champaign, Illinois, lab. Arnold supplied the drug to many athletes and many users ended up breaking records, as Montgomery did. THG was banned by the end of 2003.

Prolonged used of THG can cause infertility in men and women. Although other steroidal side effects such as acne are common with THG, THG has one unique and dangerous side effect: **immunosuppression**. Immunosuppres-sion means the body's immune system is suppressed. A state of immunosup-pression can be quite dangerous as the body becomes susceptible to infections that normally pose little threat.

Desoxymethyltestosterone (Madol)

Desoxymethyltestosterone or DMT is a steroid that was first created in 1961 by Max Huffman but was never used in the commercial pharmaceu-tical market. DMT can cause liver and heart damage when taken in high dosages.

DMT is one of Patrick Arnold's designer steroids, also known as Madol. In 2005, Patrick Arnold rediscovered DMT's anabolic potentials. DMT is much more anabolic than testosterone but not nearly as androgenic, making it a popular steroid with athletes and bodybuilders.

Arnold manufactured this drug and provided it to an American nutritional supplement company named Bay Area Laboratory Co-operative (BALCO). BALCO later became the center of one of the largest steroid scandals in U.S.

history. In addition to BALCO's products, DMT was also used in two supplements by American Cellular Labs: Tren Xtreme and Mass Xtreme. Between January 2005 and July 2009, American Cellular Labs made $5,627,361 selling thousands of bottles of Tren Xtreme and Mass Xtreme.

On January 4, 2010, DMT became a controlled substance in the United States. On January 20, 2010, American Cellular Labs pleaded guilty to a felony charge of "introduction and delivery of unapproved new drugs into interstate commerce with the intent to defraud and mislead." Even though DMT was not listed as a controlled substance until January 2010, DMT was always considered a drug, specifically a drug that had no FDA approval. It is illegal to introduce a drug into the marketplace without first getting FDA approval, which usually requires many years of research.

American Cellular Labs agreed to pay a $500,000 fine and pay for an independent lab to monitor and test its products for a five-year period.[7] Although these products previously contained DMT, Tren Xtreme and Mass Xtreme are readily available on the Internet as of 2010 at a hefty price of more than $100 per bottle. It is not clear with what American Cellular Labs may have replaced the steroids in these supplements. These products were marketed as a "potent legal alternative to steroids," and viewing the supplements on American Cellular Labs' Web site at www.americell-labs.com does not provide clear information of what this alleged legal alternative is. The history of DMT shows how easily a consumer can be deceived when buying supplements online.

Norbolethone (Genabol)

Norbolethone was created by Wyeth Laboratories in Philadelphia in the 1960s. The drug was used in clinical trials but was never manufactured for distribution due to fears of toxicity. At the time, the intent of the company was to treat children with growth problems.

Patrick Arnold, the manufacturer of other designer drugs such as the Clear, gave norbolethone a new and illegal life by manufacturing and distributing it with the intent to enhance athletic performance. This steroid was designed to avoid detection since it was a steroid that was not tested by the U.S. Anti-Doping Agency, hence the name *the Clear*. Arnold distributed the drug to San Francisco Giants slugger Barry Bonds, New York Yankees first baseman Jason Giambi, and Olympic track star Marion Jones.

Norbolethone has a stronger anabolic effect than an androgenic effect and is used by men and women. Manufacture and distribution is more limited as compared with other steroids. Users of this drug report slow and steady muscle gains. On bodybuilding message boards, users recommend using norbolethone for a cycle of eight to 12 weeks with injections taken twice a week.

Taking norbolethone does increase progesterone production in the body, which comes with unwanted side effects such as increased fat storage and breast development.

METHYLTESTOSTERONE

Methyltestosterone is an FDA-approved drug sold under the trade names Android, Testred, and Virilon. It has been diverted from the legal market and sold illegally.

Android was approved by the FDA in February 1981 to treat disorders where there is a hormone deficiency. Methyltestosterone was intended primarily to treat hypogonadism, a condition where the testes produce little or no hormones. Methyltestosterone can also be used to stimulate male puberty if onset is delayed. Steroid supplementation continues until secondary sexual characteristics such as development of body hair and deepening of the voice have occurred. Secondary sexual characteristics differentiate males from females but are not required for sexual reproduction.

Methyltestosterone can improve a variety of other disorders where the result is a lower than normal amount of testosterone in the body. Radiation treatment, for example, can cause enough damage to the body to lower hormone production.

It is important to note that people who take methyltestosterone for a legitimate medical reason take carefully monitored doses, unlike those seeking an enhanced body. In growing boys who take methyltestosterone, accelerated bone growth is a side effect. Unfortunately this spurt in growth does not match the boy's linear growth. To monitor this side effect, a doctor takes an X-ray of the hand and wrist at the onset of taking the drug and then continues to take X-rays of the hand and wrist every six months. This practice evaluates if the child's growth is normal. Steroid use is discontinued if the drug is distorting growth.

Methyltestosterone is not just for males, however. Methyltestosterone has been shown to be effective in restoring sexual energy in postmenopausal women when it is taken as part of an estrogen and progestogen therapy.[8] This finding is consistent with the relationship of sexual energy and steroids.

As indicated by the chemical name, which has the word testosterone in it, methyltestosterone was synthesized from testosterone, specifically to provide a formulation that would survive oral ingestion. Testosterone must be injected since in pill form it would be destroyed by stomach acids before it could be completely effective. Injections are not as easy or appealing as taking a pill, and therefore methyltestosterone was created.

EQUIPOISE

Equipoise, referred to as "eq" by users, is a popular steroid particularly for individuals wanting to add strength more than bulk. Equipoise is the brand name for the potent anabolic steroid boldenone undeclynate, often simply referred to as boldenone. Equipoise is manufactured by Pfizer. Equipoise is approved as an injectible for horses only.

Equipoise is a long-acting drug, meaning that there is a prolonged effect because the active ingredient is released more slowly than other steroids. In horses, Equipoise has shown to improve appetite, musculature, and hair coat. Caregivers use Equipoise when a horse is suffering from a loss of appetite from either being overworked or recovering from a disease. The long-acting aspect of the drug means only once-monthly injections are required, but it quickly improves the horse's condition. Label directions from Pfizer make it clear that this drug should not be used on humans.

In people seeking to improve their performance, Equipoise offers a strong anabolic effect and a minimal androgenic effect, which is a popular balance for most men. Despite the fact that Equipoise has never been approved for human consumption, it is still a popular drug whose users boast of gains in strength. Although Equipoise has shown a quick effect during clinical trials in horses, human users indicate that sometimes it requires three weeks to take effect. Side effects of this drug include severe acne on the back and shoulders and anxiety that some users on bodybuilding forums claim persists long after taking the drug.

Chemically, Equipoise is very similar to testosterone and Deca. Equipoise has a much more different biological effect than Deca, however, even though the two drugs are very similar. In comparison to testosterone, Equipoise has much less androgenic effect.

Equipoise breaks down in the body more slowly than other steroids. The benefit is that the drug provides a biological effect longer. For humans using the drug, the disadvantage is that the drug can be detected for a prolonged period after the user has ceased taking the drug, sometimes as long as 18 months after stopping injections.

STANOZOLOL (WINSTROL)

Stanozolol is a potent steroid and is sold in oral (Winstrol) and injectable (Winstrol Depot) form. Bodybuilders and athletes often refer to stanozolol as Winny or Winny V. Stanozolol was created by Winthrop Laboratories and approved by the FDA for human use in January 1962. Stanozolol can also be used to treat osteoporosis, specifically corticosteroid-induced

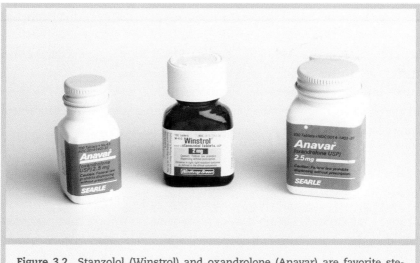

Figure 3.2 Stanzolol (Winstrol) and oxandrolone (Anavar) are favorite steroids among users for "cutting," or defining muscle tone. *(© Newscom)*

osteoporosis, and was recognized for this treatment in 1965 by the manufacturer. Stanozolol is also a veterinary steroid used in dogs and cats.

The androgenic effect of stanozolol is more mild than the anabolic effect, making the drug popular with male and female bodybuilders. Users of stanozolol usually take it with testosterone to help offset side effects such as a loss of sex drive, erectile dysfunction, depression, and moodiness. Stanozolol is regarded by many in the bodybuilding world as a strong steroid, although many users take it for a cycle of up to 12 weeks.

For individuals suffering from **Raynaud's syndrome**, stanozolol offers tremendous relief from pain. Raynaud's syndrome is a chronic condition where a person experiences episodes of decreased circulation in the hands and feet. The sufferer experiences numbness in the extremities at first and then pain and increased sensitivity. Raynaud's syndrome has been referred to as a migraine of the fingers. The loss of circulation is the source of this pain. Winstrol was approved by the FDA for the treatment of severe Raynaud's syndrome.

Stanozolol can cause liver damage that increases as the dosage increases. Since all people are biologically different, a particular amount might not cause damage in one person but cause liver damage in another person. Like many steroids, stanozolol can cause severe acne on the back and chest. The acne can become so profound that many users report using Accutane (isotretinoin), which is a FDA-approved oral drug used to treat **nodular acne**. Nodular acne originates deeper within the skin layers than normal acne and has a high chance of scarring. Accutane is a form of vitamin A, but can have serious side effects including life-threatening birth defects if a female user becomes pregnant. Females taking Accutane must agree in writing to use two forms of birth control and to get regular pregnancy tests while taking it.

NANDROLONE

In Sydney, Australia, in 2000, American shot-putter C. J. Hunter was competing in the Olympics. Hunter was the husband of Olympic track star Marion Jones. Jones and Hunter had received a lot of attention since they were expected to be the first married couple to each receive gold medals in the Olympics.

In 2000, the legal limit for the anabolic steroid nandrolone set by the International Association of Athletic Federations was two nanograms per milliliter.

As is customary before the Olympic games, Hunter was tested for steroids. His urine test revealed levels 1,000 times the allowable limit. Hunter was forced to withdraw. Hunter was later involved in a high-profile steroid scandal and divorced from Jones in 2002. Today, Hunter no longer competes athletically. Despite this example of the demise of an American Olympian, nandrolone continues to be one of the most popular steroids used today.

Nandrolone is the chemical name for one of the most common illegal anabolic steroids. It is sold under the trade name Deca-Durabolin, often referred

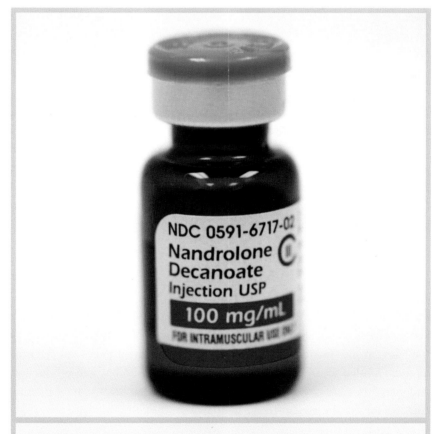

Figure 3.3 Nandrolone (Deca-Durabolin) is one of the most common illegal anabolic steroids. It works by increasing the oxygen-carrying ability of the blood. (© *Newscom*)

to simply as Deca, or a less popular formulation known as Durabolin, referred to as D-bol. Nandrolone increases the growth of certain tissues in the body and has been shown to improve the oxygen-carrying ability of blood by increasing **hemoglobin** and the size of red blood cells. Hemoglobin is a protein responsible for transporting oxygen in red blood cells.

Similar to other steroids, nandrolone causes mood swings and acne, particularly on the back. Other possible side effects include ankle swelling, breast growth, baldness, nausea, sleeplessness, vomiting, change in sex drive, and diarrhea.

Nandrolone has some legitimate medical uses such as for the treatment of osteoporosis or **anemia**. Anemia is a condition where the body does not have an adequate supply of red blood cells. Red blood cells deliver oxygen to the body. If a person is anemic, he is likely to experience fatigue, weakness, and breathlessness as his tissues are not getting sufficient oxygen. Exercise of any type would be particularly difficult since oxygen demands increase during physical exertion. Nandrolone improves an anemic condition by increasing hemoglobin and the size of red blood cells.

Nandrolone also improves bone density in women with osteoporosis. In osteoporosis the bone becomes less dense and therefore more brittle. Bones that are more brittle are more prone to breaking. Intramuscular injections of 50 mg of nandrolone every three weeks improve bone density and bone pain associated with osteoporosis.

OXYMETHOLONE (ANADROL)

Anadrol is a potent androgenic anabolic steroid in a tablet form. Anadrol is the trade name for 50 mg of the drug oxymetholone, which was developed by Syntex Pharmaceuticals in 1960. Anadrol is an anabolic steroid approved by the FDA for the treatment of anemia caused by deficient red blood cell production. Similar to other steroids, Anadrol boosts red blood cell production and therefore increases the amount of hemoglobin that helps to treat anemia. Anadrol can also be used to treat osteoporosis although drugs with fewer side effects exist.

Although Anadrol is approved for use by the FDA, the drug has serious potential side effects, such as prostate cancer in males and breast cancer in males and females. Anadrol, as well as other steroids, may cause reabsorption of the bone, a condition wherein bone cells break down bone and release the calcium to the blood. Reabsorption of the bone occurs when the body is in need of calcium. Reabsorption of the bone is serious and causes bone loss. Anadrol also poses a threat to a fetus if a woman becomes pregnant while taking Anadrol. As with many drugs, there is potential damage to the kidney since this is where the drug is processed. Because of these side effects, Anadrol is rarely used to treat osteoporosis or anemia, especially since the discovery of a drug called Epogen (epoetin alfa), which is a protein that treats these two diseases without the steroidal side effects.

Anadrol is currently used to treat HIV wasting syndrome, also referred to as AIDS wasting. HIV wasting syndrome is the loss of more than 10 percent of body weight, plus more than 30 days of either diarrhea or weakness and fever. This syndrome is not fully understood but is believed to be caused by a variety of complications involved with AIDS such as nausea, vomiting, changes in metabolism, and poor appetite.

In an experiment at the University of Düsseldorf in Germany, 89 HIV-positive men and women suffering from HIV wasting syndrome took Anadrol for 16 weeks and then were evaluated for weight gain. The study found a significant weight gain of 6.6 to 7.7 pounds during the four months. In addition, participants reported an increase in appetite, increased well-being, and reduced weakness.[9]

OXANDROLONE (ANAVAR)

Anavar is considered one of the safest steroids for women in terms of preventing unwanted masculinizing side effects and infertility. Oxandrolone is derived from DHT, similar to Winstrol and Primobolan, so it does not convert to estrogen in the body.

Oxandrolone was created by Searle Laboratories, which is now Pfizer, and was marketed under the brand name Anavar in 1964. Anavar was prescribed to promote muscle growth for people suffering from disorders that caused weight loss. Anavar also offers some improvement for women with osteoporosis.

Anavar became very popular with bodybuilders because of its strong anabolic effect and minimal androgenic effect. It is also believed to have a minimal effect on the liver. Anavar became so often abused by bodybuilders that Searle Laboratories discontinued its use in 1989, but another pharmaceutical manufacturer began marketing it under the name Oxandrin. Today, Oxandrin is made by Savient Pharmaceuticals and is prescribed to patients to promote weight gain after weight loss following extensive surgery, chronic infections, or any other disorder that makes it difficult to maintain a healthy weight. Oxandrin is also prescribed to relieve bone pain in patients with osteoporosis. Because of its potential for abuse, oxandrolone is a controlled substance under the Anabolic Steroid Control Act of 1990.

Despite this designation, bodybuilding forums boast of the gains from taking oxandrolone. The people taking oxandrolone illegally to improve appearance or performance claim it is almost five times as anabolic as testosterone but only one-fifth as androgenic. This drug is available in 2.5 mg or 10 mg tablets. Most women bodybuilders start out with three or four 2.5 mg tablets daily and, depending on the length of the cycle, work up to five or six 2.5 mg tablets daily.

The recommended clinical dose of oxandrolone is 5 mg. In clinical trials of Oxandrin, a total of 339 subjects with different underlying medical conditions took daily doses of either 5 mg or 10 mg for a maximum of four months. The research found that there was no significant difference in the ability of the patient to gain weight between the two doses.

THE EFFECTS OF CHRONIC STEROID AND PED USE

Most users of steroids follow a pattern of chronic use. Even those who elect to cycle off steroids, either for financial reasons or the unsubstantiated belief that cycling prevents long-term health problems, face the possibility of life-threatening side effects. Steroid users subject themselves to biological changes in their body, including breast tissue development, testicle shrinkage, high blood pressure, high cholesterol levels, heart disease, acne, baldness, and mood swings.

Breast Tissue Development in Men

Gynecomastia is the development of breast tissue in men. When a man takes testosterone or a **precursor** of testosterone, the body senses an overload of male sex hormone. The body will often compensate by producing estrogen.

One result of this increase in estrogen is the development of breast tissue caused by the increase in estrogen. In extreme cases, a man will even lactate.

Gynecomastia is more common with high doses of steroids. If a user does not reduce or stop steroid use, the condition can become irreversible. In some cases, a man will need to have a surgery to remove excess breast tissue.

Shrinkage of Testicles

Testosterone is produced in the testicles. When a person begins taking steroids that increase testosterone, the body responds by making less of it naturally. As a result the testicles shrink. This condition is not always reversible once a person stops taking steroids. In some cases, the testicles remain the size of raisins even after steroids have been discontinued.

High Blood Pressure and High Cholesterol

Steroid and other PED use can increase blood pressure and cholesterol levels. Blood pressure is a measurement of the pressure that circulating blood exerts on the walls of blood vessels. It is known as the silent killer because many people can have dangerously high blood pressure and not know it. Left untreated, however, high blood pressure can cause heart disease and eventually a heart attack.

Cholesterol is a waxy steroid molecule that is transported in the blood. High cholesterol can cause clogging of the arteries and contribute to heart disease. High blood pressure and high cholesterol are two risk factors for a heart attack. This is serious: heart disease is the number-one killer of men and women in the United States, according to the American Heart Association. Stopping all steroid use may see a return of pre-steroid blood pressure and cholesterol levels within a few months; however, while the individual is taking steroids, he or she is certainly at higher risk for a heart attack.

Steroid use is not just restricted to the young and fit. Many people who take steroids are trying to improve their appearance or restore their youth. It is not uncommon for individuals in their fifties take steroids, which increases the chance of a heart attack from increasing blood pressure or cholesterol, since age itself is a risk factor for heart disease.

Heart Disease

Steroids and other PEDs can damage the heart. Steroid use has been associated with **cardiomyopathy**, which is a weakening of the heart muscle. When the heart muscle weakens, then blood does not pump properly and a heart attack can occur. If a heart stops pumping then the person will die.

It is important to remember that the heart is a muscle. It is likely that the long-term use of drugs that boost muscle mass has an effect on heart muscle. Unfortunately, the science making a direct causal link is limited. Most doctors believe that steroids do in fact affect heart health, contributing to enlarged heart or **dilated cardiomyopathy**. An enlarged heart cannot pump blood efficiently.

Decreased heart function can also affect other organs in the body such as the lungs and liver. Although uncommon, cardiomyopathy can even lead to liver failure. The connection between heart failure and liver failure often goes undetected. In one reported case that was published in the *World Journal of Gastroenterology*, a 40-year-old bodybuilder showed up at a hospital with signs of liver failure, including jaundice. The man admitted to using steroids for the previous 10 years, cycling for six to 10 weeks and taking a two- to three-week break before starting another cycle. The bodybuilder said he took methandrostenolone, stanozolol, oxymetholone, nandrolone decanoate, testosterone, and trenbolone in heavy doses. For example, he took 500 mg to 700 mg of trenbolone (a long-acting steroid approved only for use on animals) per week. Due to the jaundice and past steroid abuse, the doctors initially believed that he was suffering from liver failure as a direct result of his drug use. Based on further investigation, the doctors discovered that the man had an enlarged heart, which they attributed to his steroid use. His enlarged heart and the disruption of blood flow in the body was the cause of the liver failure, proving that an enlarged heart can cause liver failure.[10] This case study shows that steroids can adversely affect multiple organs in the body at the same time.

Baldness

Baldness is caused by an interaction of enzymes and hormones. Hair grows from hair follicles. Follicles are the oblong structures within the skin that protect and mold the hair shaft. The follicle also contains a tiny muscle at the bottom that is responsible for making hair stand erect. Hair is composed of dead protein cells called keratin, whereas the follicle is made up of live cells. Hair follicles are formed very early in life—before we are even born. After birth, no more follicles are formed on the body.

Genetics, age, and testosterone levels are the main factors that determine whether someone will go bald. Scientists now believe they have isolated the gene that causes baldness. The gene, referred to as LIPH, is defective in those with baldness. The LIPH creates dihydrotestosterone (DHT). When DHT comes into contact with the testosterone in the hair follicle, it creates a by-product that dries up the hair follicle. Wherever DHT is present in the hair follicle, the hair dries up, causing the hair to grow shorter and thinner than in areas without DHT. Eventually the hair follicle becomes dormant and hair ceases to grow at all.

Steroids can cause baldness due to the increase in testosterone level. However, not all steroids will have the same effect on a user, and individual steroids vary in capacity to cause the hair follicle to dry up.

Acne

Acne is a skin condition that results from bacteria clogging the skin pores and causing blackheads, whiteheads, and pimples. Steroids disrupt the balance of hormones in the body. An increase of hormones from taking steroids can stimulate the oil glands in the skin, a process similar to that which occurs during puberty.

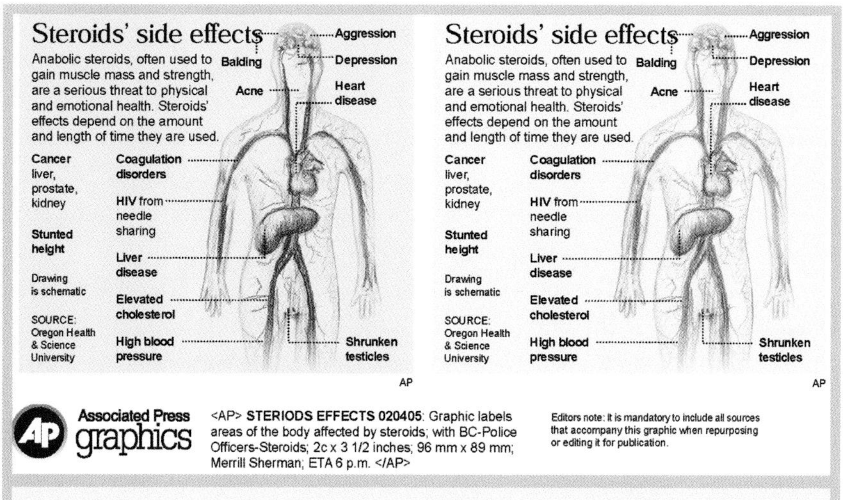

Figure 3.4 Steroid abuse can cause serious physical and emotional side effects. (© AP Images)

Acne caused by steroid use tends to be more concentrated on the back, informally referred to as "bacne." It is not well understood why acne would be more prevalent on the back, but it is known that this type of acne is more common in men and is exacerbated by sweating without adequately cleansing and exfoliating the skin.

Liver Damage

Similar to many drugs, steroids can damage internal organs, particularly the liver. The liver is responsible for detoxification in the body. For this reason, drugs are usually metabolized in the liver. The liver essentially breaks down the drug into smaller compounds to be flushed out of the body. Consistent use of any drug, even if it is taken in prescribed doses, risks damaging the liver. Oral steroids are much more likely to damage the liver than are injectables.

Although many approved drugs are tested for their impact on the liver, each person's body reacts differently to a drug and there is the possibility that a drug that does not affect one person's liver can adversely affect another person's. For people taking a daily medication that has a potential to cause liver damage, a doctor can perform a blood test to evaluate the liver's health. This blood test is called a **liver function panel**. This test evaluates blood levels of many factors, including liver enzymes.

Some medications are known to have a propensity to damage the liver. Specifically, steroids that are classified as **17-alpha alkylated compounds** can be detrimental to the liver and cause an increase in liver enzymes such as alkaline phosphatase. Damaged liver cells release increased amounts of alkaline phosphatase enzymes into the blood, and therefore if a liver function panel comes back with high levels of this enzyme, the doctor would be concerned that the drug is causing damage to the liver.

Long-term use of steroids has also been associated with liver cell tumors. Oxandrin, which is the brand name for the drug oxandrolone, comes with a boxed warning on the label letting users known that oxandrolone is associated with liver cell tumors, which can cause no symptoms until a life-threatening condition known as intra-abdominal hemorrhage develops. In addition, the label of Oxandrin also warns that this drug can cause **peliosis hepatis**, where blood-filled cysts form on the liver and can cause liver failure. Interestingly, on many bodybuilding forums, many users boast the benefits of oxandrolone, and describe the steroid as having "low toxicity," which in the enhanced performance world means that the drug is less damaging to the liver. It is unclear why steroid users would believe this since oxandrolone can be toxic to the liver.

As stated above, liver damage can progress without the user experiencing symptoms. According to the University of Iowa Hospitals and Clinics, up to 50 percent of people with liver damage experience no symptoms.[11] Many of the common symptoms of liver damage are nonspecific, meaning that they are symptoms of many other diseases, and therefore cause a delay in detection. The common symptoms include fatigue, excessive itching, and lack of motivation. The more specific, but less common, symptoms of liver disease are dark-colored urine, light-colored stool, yellowing of the eyes and skin, and retention of fluids in the abdomen.

Within a relatively short period of time, it is possible for a person to have the first signs of liver damage and proceed into liver failure. In a case study published in the *World Journal of Gastroenterology*, a bodybuilder who used steroids heavily went to the hospital after four days of loss of appetite, vomiting, abdominal pain, and yellowing of the skin.[12] In the previous month, he complained of increased fatigue, inability to keep up with his exercise regime, and general malaise. He stopped taking the steroids when he began to experience his initial symptoms but his condition did not improve. Prior to his initial symptoms, he was in good health. As it turned out, steroid-related heart damage was the cause of liver failure. This case study illustrates how a person can use steroids for many years and not have any symptoms indicating that their organs are being damaged.

Without the liver, the body cannot function. Liver damage, particularly for younger people, is a potentially life-altering condition. For individuals with a damaged liver or a disease of the liver such as hepatitis, abstinence from alcohol is recommended, since alcohol is a poison and can further damage the liver.

Fortunately, the liver is one of the organs of the body that can regenerate. When the liver is said to regenerate, it refers to the complete repair of the damage. In many cases, an organ of the body may heal, but there is not necessarily a complete healing of the organ. For example, if the skin, which is the body's largest organ, is severely injured, the body may heal, but it produces scar tissue, which is not considered regeneration.

For those who damage their body from steroid use, the liver's regenerative capabilities offer some hope. However, if a steroid user continues to use a drug that damages the liver without giving the liver time to regenerate, then the user is at a higher risk of long-term complications where the damage to the liver results in the formation of scar tissue. The development of scar tissue is generally irreversible and is referred to as cirrhosis. Heavy alcohol or drug use can cause cirrhosis of the liver that, left untreated, will cause death.

'Roid Rage

Bertil Fox is a former bodybuilder born in the West Indies. He moved to England at the age of one. After winning the Mr. World competition, Fox decided to move to the tiny islands of St. Kitts and Nevis to open his own gym after living in England for 40 years.

On September 30, 1997, Fox's former fiancée, 20-year-old beauty queen Leyoca Browne, and her mother, 36-year-old Violet Browne, were fatally shot with a gun owned by 46-year-old Fox. Fox was present at the time of the murders but denied committing them.

Fox's version of the story claims that his fiancée's mother, Violet, had the gun in her hand, pointed at Fox, at which point a struggle for the gun ensued. The first accidental shot killed Leyoca and the second accidental shot, according to Fox, killed Violet. Fox is currently serving a life sentence for the crimes in a tiny jail cell in St. Kitts. Fox is believed to be a user of steroids and his story an example of 'roid rage.

'Roid rage refers to the increase in hostility due to steroid abuse. Opinions vary considerably on how real 'roid rage is. Many users of steroids wholeheartedly discredit rage due to steroids. Gregg Valentino, a bodybuilding icon and outspoken user of steroids and other PEDs, claims that 'roid rage is a myth. He claims that if you are a jerk, steroids will make you an even bigger jerk.[13] Valentino's opinion is echoed by many users of steroids and other PEDs despite scientific evidence to the contrary.

Individuals who believe in the reality of 'roid rage point to all the unusually high numbers of bodybuilders who are behind bars for homicide, including Fox. John Riccardi is a former bodybuilder who is awaiting execution for a double homicide. Pro wrestler Chris Benoit strangled his wife and suffocated his seven-year-old son before hanging himself with his gym equipment. Benoit's long-term history of drug abuse, including steroids, came to light after his death. James Batsel, a former police officer and bodybuilder, is serving a life sentence for shooting a victim nine times.

Among those people who recognize 'roid rage as a legitimate condition, many erroneously claim that once steroids are discontinued, the resulting aggression also subsides. Unfortunately, science has shown this not to be true. According to a study at Northeastern University, long after more than 100 hamsters were taken off steroids, the aggressive tendencies continued in 85 percent of them.[14] Although this experiment involved hamsters and not humans, it provides disturbing evidence that the effects of steroids may linger beyond use and even permanently alter brain chemistry.

Discrediting increased aggression as a result of taking steroids runs counter to the general observation that altering hormones affects moods. Anabolic steroids alter hormones. It is unlikely that increasing or decreasing hormones in the body would have no effect on a person's mood, whether male or female. Many women experience a slight change in mood just before menstruation as estrogen levels dip. Denial of 'roid rage by users might have more to do with denial of a drug problem.

STEROIDS AND WOMEN

Although men have approximately 10 times more testosterone than women, women's bodies are more sensitive to an increase in testosterone or similar compounds such as steroids. For women taking steroids, the masculinizing aspects of these drugs appear more severe. Steroid use in women is far less common, but one example of a woman whose career and health were damaged is Marion Jones.

In 2000 at the Olympics in Sydney, Australia, Marion Jones won three gold medals and two bronze medals in track and field. Jones was the first woman to win five Olympic medals in this category. Jones always excelled in sports as a child. At the age of eight, she drove with her family to the Olympics in Los Angeles and proudly proclaimed to her mother that she wanted to be in the Olympics.

Despite Jones's obvious talents and hard work, she turned to PEDs to achieve her goals. In January 2008, she was sentenced to six months in prison and ordered to perform 800 hours of community service as a result of her use of PEDs and of check fraud.

Figure 3.5 Sprinter Marion Jones admitted to using performance-enhancing drugs during the 2000 Olympic Games and had to forfeit her medals. (© *Newscom*)

At the time that Jones won her medal in Sydney, her husband, Olympic shot-putter C. J. Hunter, tested positive for steroids right before the games. It is unclear whether Jones got involved with steroids through her husband, but it is clear that her involvement ruined her promising athletic career.

One disturbing and long-term effect of steroid use is the overgrowth of the clitoris. The clitoris can grow so large that it resembles a small penis. Similar to the shrinking of the testicles, this condition is generally not reversible once a woman has stopped taking steroids. Diane Williams, a former track star, admitted that her clitoris grew to embarrassing proportions when she began taking steroids.

Although steroid use is less common in women versus men, the abuse of steroids is still present with potentially devastating consequences. The use of steroids in women is less common due to steroids' unappealing side effects, which include deepening of the voice, facial hair growth, and other masculine features. For women, PED use is largely motivated by the desire to compete better rather than to look better.

EFFECTS OF HGH ON ATHLETIC PERFORMANCE

Although athletes believe that human growth hormone will increase muscles, and therefore strength, along with taking off unwanted pounds, there is little scientific evidence to support this belief. Studies evaluating the effects of HGH on healthy adults are limited. In an extensive literature review of HGH studies, the researchers found only three studies that evaluated growth hormone for longer than 30 days, and no study evaluated its use for more than three months.[15] The duration of a drug's use is important because it is possible for drugs to have a short-term effect as well as a long-term effect. Prolonged use of a drug is more likely to be associated with unwanted side effects.

Of the 44 articles on HGH that the researchers reviewed, lean body mass increased significantly in groups that were treated with HGH compared with the control group. Only two studies evaluated strength and neither one found a statistically significant increase in muscle strength. This result is remarkable given the widely held notion that HGH enhances performance. In addition, fatigue was more often reported by participants who were in the HGH group. The researchers concluded that although growth hormone may alter body composition, it has minimal effect on key athletic performance outcomes and may be associated with worsened exercise capacity.[16]

In a 2010 study published in the *Annals of Internal Medicine*, 103 healthy male recreational athletes were studied to determine if HGH improved their athletic performance. Before this study, the authors claimed there was no scientific proof that HGH does actually improve performance despite its widespread use by athletes. The authors of the paper first measured physical fitness before the subjects began taking the HGH. Specifically the subjects were assessed on their ability to pull a weight, jump, and sprint on a bicycle.

The group was then split into two groups where one group received HGH and the other received salt water injections for eight weeks. In addition, half of the men at random also received testosterone or salt water injections. The salt water injection would be assumed to not have any biological effect; it is referred to as a **placebo**. Participants who receive the placebo in any experiment are *not* told that the injection they are receiving will have no biological effect. Even though the placebo group in a study receives essentially an inert substance, there will be a response to the mere perception that they are receiving a drug. This response is referred to as the **placebo effect** and is considerable proof of the power of the mind over the body. The group receiving an inert substance will generally have a percentage of people who will have an improvement of their condition simply because they believe they are taking a drug. The placebo group is an important tool for researchers to determine exactly how much a drug is having an effect.

After the eight-week period, both groups were given the same physical fitness tests to examine improvements. They were also tested another 14 weeks after treatment to determine if gains were lasting. Growth hormone increased the athletes' ability to sprint on a bicycle but had no effects on fitness or their ability to pull a weight or jump. Testosterone injections boosted even further the ability to sprint, doubling the participant's gain in subjects that received HGH and testosterone. After six weeks of stopping treatment, however, all gains were lost. Participants who received HGH did not increase muscle mass and suffered the side effects of swelling and joint pain more than those who received the placebo.[17]

Although the ability to enhance performance may be in doubt, the seriousness of side effects is not. **Tissue edema** is a condition where fluid builds up under the skin and is a side effect of HGH use. Fatigue is also a complaint of users of HGH. Prolonged or high doses of HGH can have more serious and permanent side effects such as a thickening of the jaw and digits. Because

FACT OR MYTH: DO STEROIDS HELP ATHLETES HEAL FASTER?

Many athletes begin taking steroids after an injury to recover more quickly. Although steroids have been shown to enable the body to heal faster, the proper dosage and any necessary therapy are critical. It is widely accepted by many athletes and bodybuilders that steroids aid healing, but in fact, there are those who feel that taking steroids actually can subject the athlete to greater injury.

A former *American Gladiators* TV star, Dan Clark, asserts that injuries occur more often while a person is on steroids due to the oversized nature of the muscle. Clark suggests that when the muscle becomes too large for the bone, it is more likely to tear away from it and cause injuries such as **patellar tendinitis**. Patellar tendinitis occurs when the tendon connecting the kneecap to the shinbone is disconnected. Strained rib cages and torn hamstrings are additional injuries listed by Clark as common to steroid users, where the bulky muscle more easily tears away from the bone.

Clark also cites the number of injuries in baseball between 1992 and 2001, often referred to as the "steroid era." The number of players on the disabled list in that period rose from 352 to 465, a 32 percent increase compared with the previous 10-year period.[18]

Despite the encouragement from other users on Internet message boards to use steroids to heal from injuries, increasing the size of one's muscle far beyond what is natural likely contributes to injuries.

HGH interacts with glucose levels, insulin resistance can develop, or even type 2 diabetes. HGH can also affect other internal organs and cause acute renal failure or hepatitis.

MEDICAL USES OF HGH

HGH is used to promote growth for people with **Turner's syndrome** as well as children and adults with HGH deficiencies. In addition to promoting growth, there is some indication that HGH increases muscle mass and bone density, decreases body fat, and improves immune system function, specifically the ability to fight disease.

HGH in deficient patients also improves skin tone and texture. Because of these effects, HGH has been touted as an antiaging supplement. These effects, however, have not been documented in healthy individuals with normal HGH levels. Similar to other drugs, HGH only appears to have an effect if the individual is lacking a chemical and the drug is able to right the imbalance of the body.

Turner's Syndrome

Turner's syndrome is a genetic condition in which a female is lacking an X chromosome. Men have an XY chromosome sequence and women typically have an XX chromosome sequence. Without the proper chromosomal sequencing, girls with Turner's syndrome have many biological differences including widely spaced nipples, no menstruation, dark spots on their body, elbow deformity, and smaller fingernails. Turner's syndrome also prevents a woman from conceiving a child. Girls with Turner's syndrome also have short stature.

Treatment for Children with Short Stature

In 2003, the FDA approved somatropin, which is a growth hormone, to treat short stature in children whose height is not due to a hormone deficiency or being born premature but is likely the cause of family genetics. Somatropin is sold under the brand name Humatrope by Eli Lilly and is also labeled to treat Turner's syndrome, pediatric growth hormone deficiency, SHOX deficiency, "small for gestational age," and adult growth hormone deficiency.

Children who are short due to genetics rather than disease are referred to as having **idiopathic short stature** (ISS). *Idiopathic* means that there is no known cause, although the cause for children with ISS is likely genetics. One of the first things that most doctors ask when determining ISS is the height of the child's mother and father. Children classified as ISS are in the 1st percentile for height, meaning that out of an average group of 100 children, they would be the shortest. In terms of adult height, this roughly translates to shorter than 5'3" for a male and shorter than 4'11" for a female. The FDA's approval of somatropin is notable because it is allowing a drug to be advertised to treat a condition in children where there is no disease or disorder. Essentially, HGH is used to overcome genetic predisposition.

Research is mixed on exactly how much HGH can increase the adult height of a short stature child, but most studies show a gain of anywhere from one to three inches. But some studies indicate that the current data do not support the contention that HGH therapy improves significantly the adult height of short stature children.[19] In clinical trials performed by Eli Lilly, 71 children and teens participated in experiments where some of the children received somatropin and others received a placebo. At the onset of the 4.4 year experiment, children ranged in age from nine to 15 years old, and those in the group that received the growth hormone were given Humatrope injections three times per week. The scientists found a significant difference in height gain in the children who received Humatrope, with 41 percent of the children in the Humatrope group achieving a final height above the 5th percentile. None of the children in the placebo group reached higher than the 5th percentile.

A larger study of 239 children aged five to 15 years old was conducted by Eli Lilly to test two different doses against a placebo to determine if a higher dose of growth hormone results in greater height gains. This experiment was shorter, lasting two years, and the children and teens were either in a group that received a placebo, a 0.37 mg/kg dose per week, or a 0.24 mg/kg dose per week. The group that received the higher dosage of 0.37 mg achieved a gain of 7.2 cm (2.8346 inches). The group that received the lower dose achieved a gain of 5.4 cm (2.13 inches). Although a couple of inches might not seem like a big difference, it can be the difference between a child not being on a growth chart—meaning that they are shorter than all 100 children in a typical sample—to reaching the 5th percentile, which means that out of the sample of 100 children, they are statistically likely to be taller than four other children. In Eli Lilly's two-year study, none of the children had a height above the 5th percentile at the onset of the study. In the group that received the higher dose, 82 percent reached a height above the 5th percentile and 47 percent of participants in the lower dose group surpassed the 5th percentile for height.

Another major drawback to treating short stature with growth hormone is the expense. The cost ranges dramatically, but usually treatment starts before puberty and continues until the growth plates fuse. The cost can be $20,000 annually for a final price tag of $100,000.

Remarkably, children who take somatropin have a relatively low incidence of side effects. Because growth hormone must be taken as an injection, bruising at the injection site is one of the most common side effects. One of the less common side effects of somatropin is **intracranial hypertension**. Intracranial hypertension occurs when fluid pressure inside the skull, specifically cerebrospinal fluid, is too high. In experiments with patients taking somatropin, a small number of patients suffered from intracranial hypertension with symptoms that included headache, visual changes, nausea, and vomiting. Their symptoms subsided quickly once they discontinued use of somatropin.

INCREASING STAMINA: ERYTHROPOIETIN AND DARBEPOETIN

Erythropoietin (EPO) increases stamina because this hormone increases the production of red blood cells. In vertebrates such as people and fish, red blood cells are the main mechanism of delivering oxygen to the body. With more red blood cells, the body has more access to oxygen, and more oxygen increases the stamina of a person using a lot of it in the form of breathing—for example, a bicyclist struggling to get up a steep hill.

The dangers of EPO are an increased risk of blood clots, heart attacks, and stroke from thickening of the blood. With more red blood cells in the blood, the blood becomes more viscous (thick). A higher blood viscosity has a higher potential to clog capillaries and cause medical emergencies such as heart attack, stroke, and blood clots.

EPO became popular in competitive sports in the 1980s and continues to be popular today. Medical studies on long-term use of EPO, particularly at the doses that athletes take it, are limited or nonexistent. From 1987 through 1989, approximately 15 professional cyclists died under mysterious circumstances. Five Dutch racers died suddenly in 1987, followed by a Belgian and two Dutch riders in 1988, and five more Dutch cyclists in 1989. A number of those deaths may have been due to EPO, but the evidence is hard to come by, particularly since most athletes are secretive about using drugs for illegal purposes.[20]

MEDICAL USES FOR EPO AND OTHER RED BLOOD CELL BOOSTERS

A process known as recombinant DNA technology has created many other drugs similar to EPO that stimulate red blood cell production. Darbepoetin alfa is one of these drugs that is manufactured by Amgen under the brand name Aranesp. Darbepoetin alfa is produced in Chinese hamster ovary cells and can be mass-produced through recombinant DNA technology. Aranesp was approved by the FDA in September 2001 and is labeled to treat anemia associated with **chronic kidney disease**. Chronic kidney disease is a serious condition where the kidneys lose their ability to remove wastes and excess water from the body. A person cannot survive without kidneys. The two main causes of kidney disease are diabetes and high blood pressure.

CLENBUTEROL: IS IT JUST FOR HORSES?

Clenbuterol, commonly known as "clen," is a stimulant that is used legally as an asthma treatment for horses. It works by relaxing the muscles in the airways. Clenbuterol builds muscles, burns fat, and suppresses the appetite. Because it is a stimulant, it also speeds up the heart rate and elevates blood pressure.

The human health and safety of clenbuterol has not been well studied. Most of the data related to this drug have been on animals, and the results raise concerns. In rats, clenbuterol stiffens their hearts, causing doctors to fear that clenbuterol use in humans could increase the risk of strokes and heart arrhythmia. In Europe, clenbuterol is even banned in animals that will enter the food chain.

Even given the risks and fatalities, clenbuterol can be easily obtained over the Internet. A quick search on the Internet shows thousands of sites offering to sell clenbuterol and an equal amount of postings exchanged by bodybuilders and dieters on how much to self-administer.

Even with the FDA's approval, Aranesp has serious side effects, including cardiovascular events and stroke. Aranesp's association with adverse cardiovascular events is consistent with what has been observed with other red blood cell boosters. By increasing the number of red blood cells, the blood can become too thick for the heart to continue pumping it. For this same reason, drugs that increase red blood cells are also associated with blood clots and strokes. In addition, during clinical trials of Aranesp, patients with breast, non-small cell lung, head and neck, lymphoid, and cervical cancers had shortened overall survival or increased risk of tumor progression or tumor recurrence.

THE EFFECT OF STEROIDS AND PEDS ON WINNING

When athletes choose to take steroids, the assumption is that the gains they will make in running faster, swimming faster, hitting a ball harder, or throwing farther are worth the extra efforts and expense of taking steroids and other PEDs. But how significant is the difference?

The answer to this question is a significant one considering the controversy of using drugs to enhance performance, but is also a critically difficult one to measure. All athletes are biologically different and the effects of the same drug, even in the same dose, are likely to have a different effect from one athlete to another.

The use of steroids and other PEDs does appear to correlate with enhanced records or winning times. Patrick Arnold, the creator of designer steroids such as THG, supplied the drug to many athletes who subsequently broke records, such as sprinter Tim Montgomery.

When the East Germans incorporated their doping regime on their athletes in 1974, they won more Olympic gold medals than they ever had previously, with 40 gold medals in the 1976 Olympics; its female swimmers won 11 of 13 events.[21] In athletic competitions, seconds can make the difference between winning and losing, and steroids and other PEDs have been shown to increase the chances of breaking a record or winning.

4
Abuse, Addiction, and Treatment

I started taking anabolic steroids in 1969 and never stopped. It was addicting, mentally addicting. Now I'm sick, and I'm scared. Ninety percent of the athletes I know are on the stuff. We're not born to be 300 lb (140 kg) or jump 30 ft (9.1 m) but all the time I was taking steroids, I knew they were making me play better. I became very violent on the field and off it. I did things only crazy people do. Once a guy sideswiped my car and I beat the hell out of him. Now look at me. My hair's gone, I wobble when I walk and have to hold on to someone for support, and I have trouble remembering things. My last wish? That no one else ever dies this way.

—Lyle Alzado, NFL player

Lyle Alzado was one of the most feared defensive players in the NFL. He played for the Denver Broncos, the Cleveland Browns, and the Los Angeles Raiders from 1971 to 1985. Alzado also admitted that he abused steroids for decades and blamed them for the cancer that killed him in 1992 at the age of 43.

Alzado was born in Cedarhurst, New York, to a feisty man nicknamed Junk Yard Pat because of all the junk that filled their house, including broken appliances, rusted bikes, and car parts. Alzado's father was physically abusive to his mother and also led a secret double life with another family.

Like many steroid addicts, Alzado sought to hide the pain of his childhood through success in sports and relocating far from his childhood *home. With the help of steroids, Alzado was able to go from 190 pounds in high school to 290 while playing football at a small college in South Dakota.*

Typical of many who abuse steroids, Alzado's personal relationships suffered. His first marriage fell apart early on in his professional football career and in his second marriage he became physically abusive, just like his father. According to one account, Alzado once dragged his second wife, Cindy, out of a Broncos party and pummeled her in their car. Somehow she got control of the car and attempted to run him over. Alzado clung to the hood of her Toyota as they sped across Manhattan Beach.[1]

ADDICTION TO STEROIDS AND OTHER PERFORMANCE-ENHANCING DRUGS

About 30 percent of steroid users develop a dependence syndrome, characterized by chronic steroid use despite adverse effects on physical, psychosocial, or occupational functioning.[2]

Steroid use can become addictive, and the addiction follows a pattern similar to opioid dependence. The psychological dependence of steroids is significant for users. Withdrawal of steroids will produce fatigue, impotence, and depression. Knowing that these symptoms can be alleviated by continuing use of steroids often causes the users to choose not to take a hiatus from steroids.

Based on the reason for steroid and other PED use, many people assume users do not experience the same rush as other drugs of abuse. However, some steroid addicts claim that they can feel an immediate effect when taking high doses of steroids, which heightens the compulsion to continue taking the drug. One former addict claims that longtime users of steroids develop the ability to taste the steroids after an injection. According to this former steroid addict, "Doctors say it takes a few weeks to feel the effects of steroids. I disagree. I can taste the tinny oil the second I inject it, and I can feel it floating through my system immediately. It doesn't hit hard the way heroin does where your head drops back and you disappear into nirvana as the drug grabs you. It's more of a numbing softness that floats over me—an overall sense of well-being."[3]

Treatment centers are recognizing the hold that steroid and other PED addictions can have and have incorporated programs to treat these addictions.

STEROIDS AND OTHER PERFORMANCE-ENHANCING DRUG OVERDOSES

Although many users of steroids do not fear an overdose, it can happen. In Davenport, Iowa, a 41-year-old man died after taking Gonadotropin and Lutalyse at his home. Gonadotropin and Lutalyse are growth hormones. Lutalyse is approved for use in cows to stimulate reproduction and milk production. Just prior to his death, his temperature reached 108 degrees. His wife told the police he had just injected the steroids after purchasing three bottles from his dealer.

In another situation documented in the autobiography *Gladiator: A True Story of 'Roids, Rage, and Redemption*, Dan Clark retells a thrilling evening in 1989 that he spent with former Denver Broncos defensive end Lyle Alzado. Clark idolized Alzado as an athlete. Alzado's success also included running a Los Angeles restaurant named Alzado's. Alzado took Clark and the other Gladiators out to his restaurant, treating them to all the food and alcohol they desired. Although Alzado denied ever using steroids when interviewed on TV, Clark asked him about his steroid usage while the two were enjoying dinner and drinks at the noisy restaurant.

Clark was shocked when he heard the list of steroids that Alzado said he was taking: Equipoise, bolasterone, Winstrol, Anavar, test cypionate, and others Clark had barely heard of. Clark believed, based on his experience with steroids, that there was no way Alzado was taking all of these drugs currently. He clarified by asking Alzado what he was taking right now. "All of them," Alzado replied. "Dan, it's either go big or go home."

Inspired by Alzado's motto, Clark went home after a night of partying and lined up all of the steroids in his medicine cabinet on his bathroom sink. His cache consisted of cypionate, propionate, testosterone suspension, Primobolan, Deca, and Equipoise. First he extracted 2 milliliters of cypionate from the bottle into the syringe and then continued to extract the remaining steroids with varying amounts. In addition to the cypionate, the syringe also contained 1 ml of Equipoise, 1 ml of Primobolan, 1 ml of Deca, and 1 ml of testosterone suspension. With the remainder of the space in the syringe, Clark withdrew a whopping 6 ml of propionate even though the bottle indicated that it had expired. Clark put the syringe into his buttocks, hoping to be like Alzado one day.

Based on Clark's accounts of that night, he woke up in the middle of the night in a cold sweat with a fever and a racing heart. He vomited repeatedly, was shaking, and contemplated calling 911. He did not, however, because he did not want the public to find out that he, one of the Gladiators on TV, was taking steroids. Instead, Clark called his girlfriend Sabrina, and told her he thought he was having a heart attack.

Sabrina found Clark crumpled in the corner of his bathroom shaking and begged him to call an ambulance. Once Sabrina saw the remnants of the steroid cocktail, she headed for the phone to call a doctor. Clark begged her not to do it for fear of being discovered as a steroid user and instead asked her to just help him slow his heart down. Sabrina found a muscle relaxant, Soma, in the medicine cabinet and gave a couple of pills to Clark. Clark took more Soma and eventually he began to feel better. Sabrina decided she did not want to be a part of a steroid addict's life, and so she never saw Clark again.

EXERCISE ADDICTION: GOING OVERBOARD WITH FITNESS

The first time Amber saw Beyoncé dance on stage, she was motivated to lose a little weight and tone up. She solicited the support of her best friend, and together they ran around the block and exercised to workout videos. Amber and her friend began to feel better about themselves, but for Amber it just was not enough. Amber increased the amount that she was running and got a membership to a gym. Soon she was working out in the morning and evening without taking a single day off. Even when Amber pulled a muscle in her shoulder, she continued to work out. Her best friend told her that she was looking a little too thin, but Amber suspected she was just jealous.

Amber became addicted to exercise. Often this addiction is accompanied by an **obsessive-compulsive disorder (OCD)**, a mental disorder characterized by repetitive behaviors such as repeated hand washing, as well as

TREATMENT OF STEROID ADDICTION

At South Coast Recovery in San Clemente, California, drug and alcohol addicts enroll for a 30-, 60-, or 90-day treatment program. The treatment facility resembles a spa resort with landscaping that includes tropical flowers and palm trees, and it features group activities, including some on the beach.

South Coast Recovery is one of the few treatment centers that offer a program specifically for anabolic steroid addiction. Although anabolic steroids and other PEDs are perceived as drugs of abuse by addicts, there is still the perception that they are not as difficult to stop taking as other drugs such as heroin or cocaine.

The difficulty of an individual's drug recovery depends on a complex set of variables, such as the length of time the person has taken the drugs, his or her accustomed dosing, and the size and nature of his or her support

other compulsive behaviors, including exercise. For women, the goal of overexercising is often to get slimmer, whereas for men, it is often to appear more muscular.

Exercise addiction follows the pattern of other addictions where the individual continues the addictive behavior even though it is detrimental to his or her physical well-being and personal relationships. An exercise addict will often work out alone and cancel social events to keep up with his or her daily workout hours. In cases similar to Amber's, such addicts will even work out when they have an injury, which can be quite damaging to their health.

Exercise addiction, also referred to as gym addiction, is not recognized as a true mental disorder by the American Psychiatric Association (APA). Examples of mental disorders would be OCD or an eating disorder such as bulimia.

Although not formally recognized as a disorder by the APA, those who exercise in an addictive manner, specifically to the risk of their mental and physical well-being, will likely need counseling to correct these destructive behaviors.

network. Individuals who have taken steroids for years with few breaks will likely need support in the form of a treatment program to obtain the highest level of success.

South Coast Recovery claims to be at the forefront of treating anabolic steroid addiction and recognizes the prevalence of this addiction, particularly among teens and young adults. Often, the people who come to South Coast Recovery also struggle with abuse of alcohol and other drugs such as amphetamines. At this facility, medical professionals are available to help steroid addicts handle the withdrawal symptoms that accompany steroid withdrawal such as fatigue, restlessness, mood swings, loss of appetite, and the most dangerous side effect: depression. Depression from steroid withdrawal can be so severe that a person may commit suicide, as was the case with the Texas teen Taylor Hooton in 2003.

Another treatment facility, Sierra Tucson, in Arizona, also offers treatment for steroid addicts, although its approach differs from that of South Coast Recovery. This facility offers techniques such as acupuncture, chiropractic services, and yoga, as well as more traditional group and cognitive-behavioral therapies.

COGNITIVE-BEHAVIORAL THERAPY

Cognitive development refers to a person's ability to reason and use judgment, and his or her awareness and proper perception. When people become addicted to drugs or alcohol, their ability to properly reason is usually severely deficient.

Treatment facilities offer counseling as a critical part of recovery. In many cases, a substance abuse problem is triggered by a traumatic event. The event could be emotionally painful, such as a death or divorce, or physically painful, such as a war-related injury. Counseling helps the addict to understand his or her behavior and develop healthy coping mechanisms to stress.

Yoga is used as a method to help recover from addiction and is a form of exercise encouraged in drug and alcohol recovery centers. Yoga involves deep breathing and stretching exercises. Yoga provides an added benefit of stress reduction that is beneficial to recovering addicts, particularly those with stress-related symptoms. Although yoga has a long-standing Eastern tradition, it is growing in popularity in the West. Yoga classes are now offered at many drug treatment centers.

Recovery from steroid addiction is a long-term process and for many is a daily struggle, especially in the initial phases. Many addicts overcome one addiction only to develop another one. Once a person has become an addict, the propensity for an addictive lifestyle is stronger. Relapse is common among those in recovery and many people require a couple of stays at a rehabilitation center before they can make a permanent transition to a drug-free life.

5

Steroids, Performance-Enhancing Drugs, and the Law

The Tour de France is the extremely difficult bike race that takes place annually in July in which cyclists cover approximately 2,235 miles in three weeks. In the 2006 Tour de France, the cyclists passed through mountainous and flat terrain of six different countries: the Netherlands, Belgium, Luxembourg, Germany, Spain, and of course, France.

Prior to the start of the race, numerous riders were removed from the race for doping. American cyclist Floyd Landis won the 2006 Tour de France but was later stripped of his title after he failed a drug test at the end of the race. Landis denied using drugs and spent $2 million in the next four years trying to clear his name.

In May 2010, Landis admitted to doping since 2002 and said he did not feel guilty about taking drugs. It was a standard practice in professional cycling, he claimed, and further stated that he systematically doped with other cyclists who have never been caught, such as Lance Armstrong and Dave Zabriskie. In his confession, Landis admitted to spending $90,000 a year using blood-booster EPO, testosterone, and human growth hormone.[1] Landis claimed that most cyclists who dope, including Armstrong, avoid being caught by removing blood from their systems and reinjecting it later to boost their oxygen-carrying capacity. Landis said that he was asked by Armstrong to take care of Armstrong's blood bags while he was on vacation.

74

Armstrong, who has won seven consecutive titles at the Tour de France, strongly denied doping. Landis's confession and his allegations demonstrate how difficult steroid use in sports is to control.

LEGAL STATUS OF STEROIDS

In 1988, anabolic steroids became illegal to sell in the United States. In 1990, steroids were illegal to possess without a prescription. Enforcement of these laws is where the true challenge of steroid control lies. Although steroid laws have gotten stricter over the decades, steroid use continues.

People who use, sell, possess, or manufacture steroids can be prosecuted under federal and most state laws. The court in which the case is brought often depends on the agency responsible for the arrest and the seriousness of the charges. Many cases with potential federal jurisdiction are put in state or local courts, where sentencing may be much more severe. Even investigations begun by federal agencies such as the U.S. Postal Service are most often brought in state court, not in federal court. This is particularly true if the quantity is small and there is no indication of intent to distribute. In rare circumstances, a person can be charged in both state and federal court for the same crime.

ANABOLIC STEROID CONTROL ACT OF 1990

Federal law classified steroids as a Schedule III drug, in the same category as opium and morphine. The FDA, U.S. Drug Enforcement Administration (DEA), and American Medical Association opposed the inclusion. According to the DEA, simple possession of illicitly obtained anabolic steroids carries a maximum penalty of one year in prison and a minimum $1,000 fine if this is an individual's first drug offense. A person without a prior felony drug offense who distributes steroids can face up to five years in prison and a fine of $250,000. For a second felony drug offense, the penalties are doubled.

Even though states are governed by federal laws, they can enact their own, often stricter laws. After the Anabolic Steroid Control Act of 1990 (ASCA) was passed, for example, New York classified steroids under an even stricter category: Schedule II. Despite the unsavory consequences of getting caught using or distributing steroids, most users believe that steroid enforcement is such a low law enforcement priority that only either the very stupid or very brazen need to be concerned.[2]

ANABOLIC STEROID CONTROL ACT OF 2004

On October 22, 2004, the Anabolic Steroid Control Act of 2004 was enacted by Congress. The law specifically listed 42 compounds by their scientific name that were banned. But there are always people who will aim to circumvent the law.

Bruce Kneller was a former nurse from Massachusetts who became a designer of steroidal supplements that were not included in the list of 42 compounds banned. With Kneller's background in the medical field, he had the knowledge to tinker with the illegal steroids, changing a few molecules to create a whole new steroid. If the steroid was not listed in the Anabolic Steroid Control Act of 2004, he believed he was not doing anything illegal.

One steroid Kneller created was Halodrol. Kneller's creation came from altering a steroid named Oral-Turinabol, which was a favored drug of East Germany's Olympic team in the 1970s and 1980s. After creating Halodrol, Kneller made numerous trips to Shenzhen, China, to find a large-scale manufacturer of the drug. In 2005, Kneller found a manufacturer and began distributing Halodrol. Halodrol is illegal in the United States, but still available on the black market.

The Anabolic Steroid Control Act essentially added specific steroids to the list of illegal drugs in the United States such as cocaine and marijuana. Because of people like Kneller, new steroids are added to the list of drugs illegal to possess, use, manufacture, or distribute. Effective January 2010, three additional drugs were classified as "anabolic steroids," making them illegal to possess, manufacture, use, and distribute without a valid medical reason: boldione, desoxymethyltestosterone, and 19-nor-4,9(10)-androstadienedione. Steroids and other PEDs can be added to the list of illegal drugs based on actions by Congress.

DIETARY SUPPLEMENT HEALTH AND EDUCATION ACT OF 1994

The FDA is the agency that is responsible for protecting the public from unsafe drugs; however, the FDA has much more control over prescription drugs than it does over nonprescription drugs and dietary supplements.

Drugs that require a prescription must be supported by research to show that they are safe and effective before the FDA approves them for sale. Dietary supplements, such as bodybuilding supplements, do not have to be approved by the FDA to be sold. Manufacturers of dietary supplements must make sure, however, that their claims are not false or misleading. The FDA can intervene only after the product has reached the market and there is evidence that it is dangerous to human health.

The use of nutritional supplements in athletics is estimated at approximately 60 percent of adults and junior athletes.[3] Many manufacturers of steroid-containing supplements are creating products that contain precursors to steroids. A precursor is a chemical that changes into another substance, such as testosterone. Usually the supplement's packaging does not explain that the active ingredient will turn into testosterone once it is in the body. A 2004 study funded by the International Olympic Committee found nearly 20 percent of a sample of 240 supplements sold in the United States contained an undeclared steroid.[4]

One of the challenges of controlling the manufacture, distribution, and use of steroids is that new steroids are being created constantly. These new drugs emerge on the market without FDA approval but with serious potential for harm. A drug can be controlled only after the FDA learns of its damaging effects.

DOCTORS AND STEROIDS

In addition to buying steroids and other PEDs on the Internet or through dealers at the gym, many users get a legitimate prescription from a doctor, claiming some disorder, although the drug is to be used to enhance performance. Some doctors become well known in small bodybuilding circles as specializing in "antiaging" therapies such as HGH. Essentially, these doctors measure testosterone levels in middle-aged men, and then provide anabolic supplementation and HGH to bring these levels up to those commonly found in much younger men. One steroid user who was familiar with this method of acquiring steroids said, "It's the newest scam. If you have the cash to pay the doctors, then you can be 'on' legally."[5]

This tactic seems to be in the gray area of the law since the "patient" is getting a legal drug with a valid prescription. In addition, it is legal for a physician

HOW TO TELL IF A FRIEND IS TAKING STEROIDS OR PEDS

Taylor Hooton was a 16-year-old varsity baseball player from Plano, Texas. According to his parents, Taylor started taking steroids after his coach told him he needed to get bigger. Although being on the varsity team was impressive, Taylor yearned to be the number-one pitcher. Athletic success was of considerable significance in Taylor's hometown and in his family, where his older brother was a star and his cousin was in Major League Baseball.

His girlfriend observed him injecting steroids three times a week, and even waited in the car once while he went to meet his dealer. His parents noticed that he was volatile and moody and had him tested for drugs. He came up clean because a typical drug test does not test for steroids.

Taylor eventually quit taking steroids and became depressed, which is a common side effect of steroid withdrawal. In July 2003, Taylor's mother found him hanging from a belt in his bedroom. Taylor's

to prescribe a drug for a use other than what is listed on the label. This is referred to as an **off-label use** and is defined as a drug prescribed for a purpose not approved by the FDA. Prescribing a drug for an off-label use is legal.

REGULATION OF STEROIDS AND OTHER PEDS SOLD ON THE INTERNET

The Internet plays a pivotal role in the illegal trafficking of steroids. The Internet is a main source of steroids from countries such as China and Yugoslavia as well as detailed information on purchasing the ingredients to manufacture it.

Chronic steroid users often begin buying steroids through a dealer, frequently at a gym or through weight-lifting friends. Due to the high cost of steroids, many users begin selling steroids themselves to support their habit.

parents believe his suicide is directly attributable to depression from anabolic steroid withdrawal.

Steroids and PEDs are drugs of abuse for many teens like Taylor. It would not be uncommon for a person to hide his or her use of steroids and other PEDs to avoid criticism from non-users.

The most obvious clue to steroid use is rapid weight gain and musculature. A 10- to 20-pound gain of solid muscle would be a warning sign. Another sign is an outbreak of acne on the back and chest. Certain steroids increase sebaceous (i.e., oil) gland activity. This extra oil combines with dead skin and bacteria to clog the pore and cause a pimple.

Steroid users will often experience unexplained mood swings and have bouts of aggression, and yet be in denial that they have a problem. In many cases, the addict may retreat from social activity to escape criticism.

Boys who are involved in athletics or who are overly concerned with their appearance, particularly the bodybuilding image, tend to be at higher risk of taking steroids or PEDs. Keeping all of these factors in mind, approaching a friend to express concern could save a life.

Many Internet sites sell the raw materials to make steroids and other PEDs or already manufactured drugs. Many of these Web sites boast of their discretion in shipping to prevent interception in customs. The sender usually does not print a company name on the outside or any other information that would alert customs to the contents. Packages are also kept smaller and orders are shipped in multiple packages if necessary. One steroid user reported receiving his steroids within a few days of his order wrapped in brown paper with nothing printed on the exterior. When he opened the package, there was a single VHS tape inside. After taking the shrink-wrap off the tape, he found all of the drugs he ordered taped neatly inside.

The FDA periodically inspects packages at ports of entry to make sure they do not contain illegal drugs or unapproved drugs. It is illegal to purchase either type of drugs over the Internet, or to purchase approved prescription drugs without a prescription. The FDA has the right to inspect packages and either return or destroy illicit drugs. Owners of Web sites understand these restrictions and try to find ways to get through United States customs, and also protect the buyer from prosecution.

Purchasing drugs over the Internet can be dangerous because the drug could be counterfeit or the wrong drug. The FDA is periodically alerted to such frauds and attempts to warn the public through press releases and their Web site; however, it is truly "buyer beware" when it comes to buying drugs over the Internet.

Assuming that the steroid or other PED purchased via Internet is correctly labeled, the savings for a steroid user can be considerable. The price of buying steroids or other PEDs over the Internet can often be one-fourth or less of what it is by buying them from a dealer in the United States.

HOME BREWING

Home brewing is an illegal practice of small-scale steroid manufacturing. Despite the consequences, many steroid users home brew to support their habit by selling these homemade drugs to make additional money. Home brewing is perceived by many as a safer route to acquiring steroids than purchasing over the Internet and possibly getting caught by U.S. customs or the post office.

Steroids that are available for veterinary use are more easily home brewed because of the availability of the raw compounds. One example is trenbolone, which is commonly referred to as tren. Trenbolone is used by veterinarians on livestock to increase appetite and muscle growth. Because it is used for legitimate purposes on animals, Tren can be purchased at any farm supply store without a prescription.

Tren from a farm supply store comes in the form of pellets that are shot into the back of the animal's ear with an implant gun. To get the drug out of the pellet, another product has to be used to separate the steroid from the implant pellet. And this is how, once again, the Internet is a tool for people to abuse steroids.

In the case of Tren, kits can be purchased on the Internet to alter the pellets. To hide the intent of the product, one Internet site refers to these products as "aromatherapy kits." The Internet has a variety of sites that sell these kits in 2 gram, 4 gram, 6 gram, 8 gram, and 10 gram sizes, depending on the volume of steroids to be manufactured.

The kits contain a chemical that is added to the pellet that subsequently reveals multicolored layers that expose the steroid. The maker uses a syringe and a syringe filter to extract the steroid and place it in another vial with a small amount of oil. The solution is then sterilized by cooking it in the oven.

Home brewing is quite lucrative, with one user claiming he can buy $1,500 in materials, not including the lab materials such as beakers and crimpers, to produce $50,000 worth of steroids.

One of the many dangers of purchasing steroids or any other drug from a home brewer is that the likelihood of contamination or improper preparation is much higher than purchasing a drug from a pharmaceutical company. It is safe to assume that most home brewers of steroids and other PEDs have little to no training when it comes to chemistry or making drugs. In addition, there is no way of accounting for the proper preparation or sterilization of home brewing equipment.

Certified laboratories in the United States must adhere to certain operating procedures to make sure their drugs are properly and safely prepared. Beakers are sterilized and equipment is calibrated to make sure that measuring devices are functioning properly. It is highly unlikely that home brewers are calibrating equipment just as certified labs are required to do. Using equipment that is not properly calibrated can lead to errors in measuring samples.

In general, however, people who buy from home brewers often blindly trust their source. According to one female buyer of home brewed steroids, "I never questioned it. I knew the guys . . . they were the ones helping me with my diet and everything and I just never gave a second thought about getting caught or anything. Sorta just like going to the doctor . . . they'd tell me what I needed and what to take as I got closer to my show . . . and they would have it for a reasonable cost. It's not hard at all."[6]

STEROIDS AND COUNTERFEIT DRUGS

In Mexico, steroids can be purchased over the counter at a pharmacy. Mexico is well known as a source for drugs that are illegal in the United States and for prescription drugs that can be bought without a prescription, such as Retin-A, a prescription drug used to control acne. A great proportion of Mexican pharmacies reside near the U.S. border, presumably to cater to American customers. Many athletes and others seeking to purchase steroids and other illegal or prescription drugs drive to these towns with the specific purpose of buying these drugs.

CREATINE: HEALTHY OR DANGEROUS?

Creatine is a popular and legal supplement used by bodybuilders, athletes, and anyone wishing to add muscle. Creatine is synthesized naturally in the body from **amino acids**, which are the building blocks of protein. Although creatine is stored primarily in the muscles, it is not created there. Creatine is produced in the kidneys. In addition to synthesis, creatine can also be obtained directly from food, primarily from red meat, fish, and to a limited extent in cranberries. Creatine's role in the body is to supply energy to muscles and to the brain. The majority of creatine in the body is found in skeletal muscle.

The amount of creatine taken in supplements is usually the equivalent or more of what would occur in a diet high in red meat. One pound of beef contains about 5 grams of creatine. Many creatine supplements contain 1 to 5 grams of creatine per serving, with many people taking multiple supplements throughout the day.

According to the Mayo Clinic, approximately 25 percent of professional baseball players and up to 50 percent of professional football players consume creatine supplements.[7] Creatine is more popular among athletes who gain more from muscle size than endurance, as do cyclists or swimmers. For many people who take creatine, however, the motivation is simply vanity.

Due to its popularity, creatine is sold in numerous supplements under the following names, some less obvious than others: beta-GPA, Challenge Creatine Monohydrate, Cr, creatine monohydrate powder, creatine ethyl ester, Creatine Monohydrate Powder, creatine phosphate, Creatine Xtreme Punch, creatinine, Creavescent, cyclocreatine, Hardcore Formula Creatine Powder, HPCE Pure Creatine Monohydrate,

In the United States, the FDA is responsible for making sure that drugs are safe for the American public. When Americans purchase illegal drugs in other countries, they are putting their health at risk. The FDA attempts to control the flow of anabolic steroids to the United States at ports of entry. If an

methyl guanidine-acetic acid, methylguanidine-acetic acid, N-amidinosarcosine, N-(aminoiminomethyl)-N methyl glycine, Neoton, Phosphagen Pure Creatine, Monohydrate Power Creatine, Runners Advantage creatine serum, Total Creatine Transport. Although creatine is synthesized in the body, most supplemental forms are created in a lab and not derived from animal sources, which makes them acceptable for vegetarians.

According to the Mayo Clinic, several high-quality experiments have shown that creatine can increase muscle mass. As with many drugs, however, any compound has a different biological effect from person to person. For individuals who have naturally high creatine or who already consume a diet high in red meat, creatine is less likely to lead to a significant gain in muscle. For a vegetarian, however, who is more likely to have lower creatine levels, creatine supplements generally will increase their creatine levels in the body and may lead to an increase in muscle mass if the user works out in a manner consistent with building muscle.

According to the Mayo Clinic, creatine can help build muscle; however, as with any drug, side effects do exist. The most serious side

effects involve kidney, liver, and heart damage. Liver damage is also possible, but more likely with those who have a compromised liver or kidneys. On bodybuilding message boards, many creatine users complain of extreme thirst, with one user complaining that he wakes up every hour during the night needing to drink water. Many users indicate that this side effect subsides after continued use and increasing water consumption.

American chooses to go to Mexico or smuggle it in, there is no guarantee that the drug will be safe to take. On bodybuilding message boards, steroid users admit to purchasing anabolic steroids in Tijuana, but then acknowledge their suspicions that the product is counterfeit or expired.

OPERATION RAW DEAL

To date, the largest steroid law enforcement action was a federal initiative called Operation Raw Deal that culminated in 2007. The event resulted in 124 arrests and the seizure of 56 steroid labs across the United States. In total, 11.4 million steroid dosage units were seized, as well as 532 pounds (242 kilograms) of raw steroid powder of Chinese origin. As part of Operation Raw Deal, $6.5 million was also seized, as well as 25 vehicles, three boats, 27 pill presses, and 71 weapons.[8]

Operation Raw Deal took years to orchestrate and required the cooperation of many agencies, including the FDA, DEA, and the U.S. Postal Service, as well as agencies in Mexico, Canada, China, Belgium, Australia, Germany, Denmark, Sweden, and Thailand. Operation Raw Deal struck at the core of the underground steroid manufacturing and distribution network that often begins with raw materials produced in unsanitary conditions in China that make their way to the United States.

The strategy of Operation Raw Deal was described as a four-pronged approach that focused first on raw material suppliers in China and other countries. Many home brewers of steroids purchased their raw materials from China. The second target was anabolic laboratories in the United States, Canada, and Mexico. In many cases, anabolic laboratories are large-scale operations.

Operation Raw Deal also shut down U.S.-based Web sites that provide products used to convert the raw material to a usable steroid. One of these Web sites sold "aromatherapy kits" that consisted of chemicals to break down trenbolone pellets. (Although these conversion kits do not contain steroids, they are a vital part of the illicit steroid market.) And lastly, the many bodybuilding Web sites that offer an open forum to discuss steroids and provide guidance for manufacturing steroids were also part of enforcement actions.

Californian Adam C. Hullander was one of the people arrested as a result of Operation Raw Deal. Hullander ran an Internet-based company called

Tweak Labs that sold anabolic steroids and other illegal drugs. Hullander ordered raw materials from countries such as China to make anabolic steroids. Hullander used bodybuilding Web sites such as www.anabolicboard .com to market his products. It was evident that Hullander knew that his operations were illegal and as a result he used encrypted e-mail services such as Hushmail to reduce his chances of getting caught. If a customer wanted to order steroids through tweaklabs.com, the individual would send an e-mail to tweaklabs@hush.com.

From April 2005 to April 2007, Hullander sold 16 different kinds of steroids totaling more than one kilogram, which equates to approximately 40,000 units. A unit of steroids is 0.5 ml that is distributed in pill, capsule, and

Figure 5.1 Operation Raw Deal culminated in 2007 with 124 arrests and the seizure of 56 steroid labs across the United States. (© *Drug Enforcement Administration*)

tablet form. For other forms of steroids, such as liquid, 25 mg of a steroid is considered one unit. Hullander's inventory included trenbolone, Nandrolone Deca, and Anadrol. Customers were asked to pay by Western Union money transfer. The reason Hullander asked for a money transfer was to avoid creating a paper trail, once again hiding his illegal activities. Despite Hullander's efforts to hide his earnings from selling steroids, the U.S. government was able to track down at least $81,000 that was later confiscated. In total, Hullander was charged with conspiracy to import anabolic steroids, conspiracy to distribute steroids, and conspiracy to launder money. Each charge is punishable by more than one year in prison.

OPERATION GEAR GRINDER

"Ladies and gentleman, we're here to eradicate Mexican steroids," DEA agent Jack MacGregor announced to a roomful of other agents on March 29, 2004, in San Diego. MacGregor had already begun organizing one of the largest Mexican investigations of steroid production, named Operation Gear Grinder. To keep him motivated about the importance of his mission, MacGregor kept a photo in his office of Taylor Hooton, the teenager who committed suicide after quitting steroids.

In the meeting, MacGregor displayed satellite photos of labs in Mexico that he wanted to target. MacGregor knew the names of the men who owned them and the steroids they produced.

One of the companies that MacGregor targeted was Quality Vet, which also went by the names of Denkall and Animal Power. These manufacturers were top producers for Nandrolone. The owners, Alberto Saltiel-Cohen, Joaquin Garcia Rivas, and Javier Garcia de la Pena, tried to make it seem that the products they were selling were strictly for animal use. Because steroids are legal to manufacture for animal use, the enforcement action was required to prove that the makers intended to produce the steroids for human use. Alberto Saltiel-Cohen was a savvy criminal who had been trained as a veterinarian in California. Cohen's three Mexico City–based labs represented an alarming 70 percent of all the Mexican steroids produced that were shipped to the United States from his Web sites.

Saltiel-Cohen was reported to have lived a modest lifestyle despite his estimated multimillion-dollar profits from selling steroids from his three labs.

Despite the fact that Cohen's three Web sites displayed cute animals and he tried to make it look like his products were strictly for animal use, the DEA went undercover by having agents send e-mails to order products shipped directly to people instead of veterinarians; veterinarians would be the likely recipients if the products truly were intended for animals. Saltiel-Cohen's three companies pleaded guilty to conspiracy to distribute controlled substances and aiding and abetting international monetary transactions. In the end, Saltiel-Cohen, a resident of Mexico, forfeited $1.4 million to the U.S. government.

Operation Gear Grinder revealed that, as suspected, the majority (82 percent) of steroids in the United States originate in Mexico. This 82 percent of all steroids from Mexico and used in the United States is the product of just eight companies that Operation Gear Grinder exposed. According to the DEA, the estimated combined total of annual sales from these eight companies was $56 million.

Operation Gear Grinder and Operation Raw Deal have set a great example of how the states and the federal government intend to enforce steroid laws. Many steroid users mention these actions as a reason that they have altered their behavior for fear of being caught. For any of the laws regarding steroids and other PEDs to have impact, similar initiatives will need to continue.

6

Future Trends of Steroids and Other Performance-Enhancing Drugs

In MTV's popular reality show Jersey Shore, *four men and four women are filmed spending their summer at the beaches of Seaside Heights. The eight cast members flaunt their bodies at the beach and boardwalk during the day and in the clubs in the evening. Two of the male cast members, Ronnie and Mike (a character who goes by the name "The Situation") have particularly muscular physiques.*

Ronnie and The Situation are extremely muscular, and the plethora of on-air bar fights have led to speculation that the two are using steroids. Twenty-three-year-old Ronnie, who is 5'5" and weighs 220 pounds, denies allegations that he is taking steroids. "I've taken supplements over the counter and ordered stuff online, but never steroids," he said. "You don't have to be on steroids to look good. It's about what you eat." Off the record Ronnie said, "You do what you gotta do."[1] Despite his denials, bodybuilder Web sites continue to doubt that Ronnie's physique could be simply a matter of diet. In addition, it is possible that products ordered over the Internet touted as bodybuilding supplements may have nearly the same biological effect as anabolic steroids.

Looking muscular can be quite lucrative even if those muscles are only for looks. Ronnie and The Situation have received appearance gigs and endorsement deals from the fitness industry, unlike their two other male cast mates, who appear trim and in shape but are without bulging muscles. According to the Huffington Post, *The Situation earned $5 million in 2010, from his $60,000 per episode of* Jersey Shore, *appearance fees ranging from $15,000 to $50,000, and endorsements including workout videos.*[2]

With ordinary people reaching fame through essentially appearance alone, it is no wonder that many young people reach for steroids and other PEDs. Even if Jersey Shore *seems like an inane, innocuous show, it reaches many young people with an average viewership of 2.7 million viewers in its first season in 2009 and 5.252 million viewers in its second season. The popularity of an overly muscled physique has clearly been a boon to the steroid and supplement industry.*

STEROID EDUCATION AND OUTREACH: LOCAL TO INTERNATIONAL

In October 2009, the Chicago Bears football team sponsored an event for Chicago-area high school athletes to promote nutritional techniques as an alternative to steroids. Outreach efforts such as this one are part of a steroid prevention program: Athletes Training and Learning to Avoid Steroids (ATLAS).

A strategic steroid education program aimed at high school and college students is critical to reverse the trend of increasing steroid use in teens. Taking steroids can become just as damaging and addictive as any other illegal drug. Following the lead of other antidrug campaigns, ATLAS encourages parents to talk to their children about the dangers of steroid use, particularly if their child is in a high-risk group, such as a participant in team sports, or is overly concerned about personal appearance.

Many anti-steroid experts recommend mandatory testing starting as early as high school to prevent steroid abuse early on. Steroid use in teen years is a strong predictor of abuse of steroids later in life. In addition, teens who abuse steroids are generally more willing to dabble in the abuse of other illegal drugs.

ERADICATING MISCONCEPTIONS

One of the most difficult aspects of preventing steroid use is the widespread belief by many users that steroids are not detrimental to one's health, particularly if you take a break every once in a while, a practice known as "cycling."

In a study published in 2008 by Southern Illinois University, 37 recreational steroid users were interviewed about their use and perceptions about steroids. Despite all the scientific evidence available from medical experts that shows the detrimental side effects of steroids, all the men interviewed had only minimal or, more often, no concern about steroid use on their health. One steroid user said, "I've been taking steroids for eight years and I have three kids and a full head of hair. As long as you know what you're doing, steroids are going to help you, not hurt you. The government is just totally wrong when it comes to drugs, so I don't pay attention to their hype."[3]

One of the other reasons for steroid and PED use is how these products are marketed as natural and safe. Although many of the ingredients in supplements can be just as dangerous as steroids, the labeling can be misleading. In 2006, a 24-year-old swimmer from Kentucky who had taken a supplement with 19-norandrosterone tested positive for steroids and was disqualified. The swimmer claimed that he had no knowledge that the supplement contained a prohibited drug and sued the manufacturer. He was awarded $578,635. Although the

BUILDING MUSCLES NATURALLY

Enhancing strength through diet and exercise is a core component of optimal health. Increasing strength requires developing muscles. A toned physique is aesthetically appealing and also offers numerous health benefits.

Muscle mass helps to boost the burning of fat. People with a higher percentage of muscle generally burn more calories at rest, referred to as a basal metabolic rate, than they would with less muscle mass.

Maintaining muscle mass through strength training also offsets the effects of aging. As people age they lose muscle mass, as the ability of the body to convert food to muscle decreases and the body's ability to prevent muscle breakdown decreases. A loss of muscle reduces strength and makes a person more susceptible to falls. Muscle loss also reduces basal metabolic rate and therefore leads to weight gain often associated with aging. For women, muscle mass helps percentage of people who unknowingly take PEDs is perhaps a minority, the presence of these drugs in other substances is a public health risk.

INTERNATIONAL EFFORTS

Due to the nature of athletic competitions, an international effort is critical to controlling doping in sports and educating others about the dangers of PEDs. In 1999, one of the most influential international anti-doping agencies was established: The World Anti-Doping Agency (WADA). To the chagrin of many athletes, WADA, headquartered in Montreal, is the agency that develops international anti-doping policies, referred to as the World Anti-Doping Code. WADA's efforts also include scientific research and outreach. One of WADA's outreach efforts includes a program called the Athlete Outreach Model, whereby an athlete can pass along the anti-doping message. This program includes an interactive computer game called The Play True Quiz, templates for anti-doping banners, and other publications.

prevent bone loss due to osteoporosis. Muscle is more dense than fat and helps to compact the bone.

Certain kinds of exercise increase strength. Exercise enables the muscle cells to get bigger. The number of muscle fibers, however, cannot be increased through exercise; only the size of the muscle cells can be increased. The same is true for fat cells. Each person has a certain number of fat cells. Diet and exercise can reduce the size of the fat cells but cannot reduce their number.

Muscles are developed in the body by food and exercise. Without sufficient caloric intake, the body will not be able to build muscle. A diet with plenty of protein is believed by many experts to promote muscle growth while strength training.

The best diet and exercise program to build muscles naturally will depend on a person's goals. An athlete or bodybuilder will

likely be seeking to add muscle to help prevent osteoporosis and tone up will likely drop some of the fat from his or her diet.

Figure 6.1 World Anti-Doping Agency (WADA) president John Fahey speaks in 2009. Established in 1999, WADA develops international anti-doping policies. *(© AP Images)*

INTERNATIONAL DRUG TRAFFICKING TRENDS

Anabolic steroids are illegal in the United States but are not illegal in many other countries. A common way for people to acquire steroids is to have them imported from countries where the manufacture and sale of steroids is legal. Although it is still illegal to import steroids to the United States, it remains a common method for users to acquire their drugs.

The international community recognized the growing trend of drug trafficking through the Internet and responded with the creation of the International Narcotics Control Board (INCB). Along with other agencies, the International Criminal Police Organization (INTERPOL), which is an organization comprising 186 countries, launched Project Drug.net to tackle the purchase, sale, and production of prescription drugs and anabolic steroids through the Internet. The project organized a number of training workshops and published a training manual to halt the flow of illegal drugs across borders.

GENE DOPING

One of the biggest challenges to controlling the abuse of steroids and PEDs is the ever-expanding list of drugs. Each time a new PED is synthesized, it must be added to the list of controlled substances and be incorporated in education and outreach efforts. In the increasingly complex world of PED synthesis, athletes and others seeking to enhance their performance have found a way to inject genetic material that has an effect similar to a PED but is much more difficult to prove.

Gene doping is the name of this newer method of enhancing performance and is defined as the transfer of genetic material, such as a virus, to enhance performance. The performance-enhancing virus would attach itself to a structure on the host's (i.e., athlete's) cell. This structure is known as the cell receptor. Once the virus attaches to the cell receptor, it can change the behavior of the cell. This change leads to a response in the body very similar to the ingestion of a steroid or other PED. One example of gene doping would be that the genetic material causes an increased production of red blood cells. In short, the athlete becomes the source of his own steroid or other PED.

The biological mechanism of gene doping is very similar to taking other drugs that enhance performance. When a steroid, for example, is present in the body, it attaches to the receptor within the skeletal muscle cell and alters the behavior of the cell, specifically increasing protein synthesis within the skeletal muscle cell to increase the size of the cell, thus making a person's muscle larger. This technique was originally developed to treat diseases caused by gene defects such as cystic fibrosis and muscular dystrophy.

Gene doping is a more complicated process than taking oral or injectable drugs or even blood doping. Some experts believe it would take a coordinated governmental effort to successfully use gene doping in its athletes. This notion may seem far-fetched, but given the history of steroids and East Germany, it is obviously not impossible.

In a documentary, a Chinese doctor is caught on film offering stem-cell therapy to a reporter posing as an American swimming coach. The doctor offers the treatment to the American for $24,000 and the doctor is quoted as saying, "We have no experience with athletes here, but the treatment is safe and we can help you. It strengthens lung function and stem cells go into the bloodstream and reach the organs. It takes two weeks. I recommend four intravenous injections . . . 40 million stem cells or double that, the more the better. We also use human growth hormones, but you have to be careful because they are on the doping list."[4]

The World Anti-Doping Agency and the International Olympic Committee banned gene doping in 2003, yet at the time there was not a practical test to determine if an athlete had gene doped. In 2010, through funding by WADA, scientists developed a conventional blood test to detect gene doping, even if the doping occurred as much as 56 days earlier. The test determines whether **transgenic DNA** is present in blood samples. All cells contain DNA; however, transgenic DNA is genetic material that comes from another species.

Keeping pace with doping athletes is a formidable and expensive task. It took four years of research and $980,000 to develop the test to detect gene doping.

NEW TECHNIQUES AND TECHNOLOGIES IN ANTI-DOPING TESTING

In a 2007 interview at the Aspen Ideas Festival, in Colorado, Lance Armstrong opined that the best way to control doping in sports would be to have **out-of-competition testing**, where athletes must report their whereabouts every day of the year and be able to provide a sample for drug testing if an anti-doping agency requests it. Out-of-competition testing is a control mechanism meant to catch athletes who dope intermittently, stopping before a competition so that any PEDs will clear from their system. Out-of-competition testing would be an excellent tool to prevent doping. However, testing all athletes periodically throughout the year is a labor-intensive process.

CONCLUSION

The abuse of steroids and other PEDs is rapidly changing, perhaps more so than most other drugs of abuse such as alcohol, cocaine, or heroin. When steroids first came on the market, there were only a few available. Today, there are thousands of steroids and PEDs available for abuse. Determining who is and is not doping in professional sports is an ongoing effort by WADA and other agencies.

Steroids and other PEDs have been well documented to enhance athletic performance by increasing muscle mass or red blood cell production. With thousands of dollars at stake in endorsement deals for winners, as well as the public's desire to look good, the ever-evolving black market of steroids continues to thrive.

Although the number of deaths associated with steroids and other PEDs is not as high as for other drugs of abuse, such as alcohol, detrimental side effects are well documented. Long-term effects of steroids still remain unclear, as there have not been any published studies in peer-reviewed journals determining the effects of decades of steroid and other PED use.

Despite the potential for abuse, steroids and human growth hormone are valuable drugs to treat hormone-related disorders, Turner's syndrome, osteoporosis, and HIV wasting disease, and to restore sexual function in postmenopausal women. For individuals with these diseases, steroids and HGH offer relief. As with many drugs, the balance between creating drugs to cure diseases and preventing diversion for illicit purposes is a challenge for medicine and organizations such as the FDA that are meant to protect the public's health. For individuals who benefit from these drugs, the challenge is certainly worthwhile.

NOTES

Chapter 1

1. Dan Clark, *Gladiator: A True Story of 'Roids, Rage, and Redemption* (New York: Scribner, 2009), 5.
2. 2010 Drug Policy Alliance, "Steroids," *Drug by Drug*, http://www.drugpolicy.org/drugbydrug/steroids (accessed June 28, 2010).
3. William N. Taylor, M.D., *Anabolic Steroids*, 2nd ed. (Jefferson, N.C.: McFarland and Company, 2008), 31.
4. F. Kadi, "Cellular and molecular mechanisms responsible for the action of testosterone on human skeletal muscle," *British Journal of Pharmacology* 154 (2008): 525.
5. Taylor, *Anabolic Steroids,* 32.
6. Tony Newman, "Who Among Us Isn't Enhancing Their Performance?" *Huffington Post*, http://www.huffingtonpost.com/tony-newman/who-among-us-isnt-enhanci_b_77931.html (accessed October 18, 2010).
7. Gen Kanayama et al., "Anabolic-androgenic Steroid Dependence: An Emerging Disorder," *Addiction* 104, no. 12 (2009): 1966.
8. Bridget M. Kuehn, "Teen Steroid, Supplement Use Targeted: Officials Look to Prevention and Better Oversight," *Journal of the American Medical Association* 302, no. 21 (2009): 2301.
9. Kuehn, "Teen Steroid, Supplement Use Targeted," 2002.

Chapter 2

1. Daniel M. Rosen, *Dope: A History of Performance Enhancement in Sports from the Nineteenth Century to Today* (Westport, Conn.: Praeger Publishers, 2008), 12.
2. Rosen, *Dope*, 23.
3. Domhnall Macauley, "Doping in Sport—A Warning from History," *BMJ* 335, no. 7620 (September 20, 2007): 618.
4. Timothy Jon Curry and Matthew A. Salerno, "A Comment on the Use of Anabolic Steroids in Women's Olympic Swimming: A Chronicle of the 100-Meters Freestyle," *International Review*

for the Sociology of Sport 34, no. 2 (1999): 175.

5. Steven Ungerleider, *Faust's Gold: Inside the East German Doping Machine* (New York: St. Martin's Press, 2001), 1–2.

6. Rosen, *Dope*, 46.

7. Alan D. DeSantis, *Inside Greek U.: Fraternities, Sororities, and the Pursuit of Pleasure, Power, and Prestige* (Lexington: University Press of Kentucky, 2007), 213.

Chapter 3

1. Clark, *Gladiator*, 123–131.

2. Matthew Petrocelli, Trish Oberweis, and Joseph Petrocelli, "Getting Huge, Getting Ripped: A Qualitative Exploration of Recreational Steroid Use," *Journal of Drug Issues* 38, no. 4 (2008): 1187–1205.

3. Taylor, *Anabolic Steroids,* 59–64.

4. F. Hartgens, H. Kuipers, J. A. Wijnen, and H. A. Keizer, "Body Composition, Cardiovascular Risk Factors and Liver Function in Long-term Androgenic-anabolic Steroids-Using Bodybuilders Three Months After Drug Withdrawal," *International Journal of Sports Medicine* 17, no. 6 (1996): 429–433.

5. Matthew Petrocelli, Trish Oberweis, and Joseph Petrocelli, "Getting Huge, Getting Ripped: A Qualitative Exploration of Recreational Steroid Use," *Journal of Drug Issues* 38, no. 4 (2008): 1187–1205.

6. Philip Hersh, "A New Fastest Human at 9.78: Montgomery Sets 100-meter Mark," *Chicago Tribune*, September 15, 2002, http://articles.chicagotribune.com/2002–09-15/sports/0209150475_1_trevor-graham-world-records-meters (accessed October 15, 2010).

7. Michael O'Keeffe and Nathaniel Vinton, "American Cellular Labs Pleads Guilty to Selling Anabolic Steroids Tren, Madol," New York *Daily News*, January 20, 2010, http://www.nydailynews.com/sports/more_sports/2010/01/20/2010–01-20_american_cellular_labs_pleads_guilty_to_selling_the_anabolic_steroids_tren_and_m.html (accessed September 20, 2010).

8. S. R. Lenharo Penteado et al., "Effects of the Addition of Methyltestosterone to Combined Hormone Therapy with Estrogens and Progestogens on Sexual Energy and on Orgasm in Postmenopausal Women," *Climacteric* 11, no. 1 (2008): 17–25.

9. Ulrich R. Hengge et al., "Oxymetholone for the Treatment of HIV-Wasting: a

Double-Blind, Randomized, Placebo-Controlled Phase III Trial in Eugonadal Men and Women," *HIV Clinical Trials* 4, no. 3 (May/June 2003): 150–163.

10. Miguel Bispo et al., "Anabolic Steroid-induced Cardiomyopathy Underlying Acute Liver Failure in a Young Bodybuilder," *World Journal of Gastroenterology* 15, no. 23 (June 21, 2009): 2920–2922.

11. Douglas LaBrecque, M.D., "Liver Disease: Frequently Asked Questions," University of Iowa Healthcare, http://www.uihealthcare.com/topics/medicaldepartments/internal medicine/liverdisease/index.html (accessed August 20, 2010).

12. Miguel Bispo et al., "Anabolic Steroid-induced Cardiomyopathy Underlying Acute Liver Failure in a Young Bodybuilder," *World Journal of Gastroenterology* 15, no. 23 (June 21, 2009): 2920–2922.

13. Nathan Jendrick, *Dunks, Doubles, Doping* (Guilford, Conn.: Lyons Press, 2006): 189.

14. Jeanie Lerche Davis, "Steroids May Alter Aggression Area of Brain," *WebMD Health News*, http://www.webmd.com/mental-health/news/20031126/steroids-may-alter-aggression-area-of-brain (accessed July 20, 2010).

15. Hau Liu et al., "Systematic Review: The Effects of Growth Hormone on Athletic Performance," *Annals of Internal Medicine* 148, no. 10 (May 20, 2008): 750.

16. Liu et al., "The Effects of Growth Hormone on Athletic Performance," 754.

17. Udo Meinhardt et al., "The Effects of Growth Hormone and Body Composition and Physical Performance in Recreational Athletes: A Randomized Trial." *Annals of Internal Medicine* 152, no. 9 (May 4, 2010): 568–577.

18. Clark, *Gladiator*, 235.

19. C. J. Elder et al., "A Randomised Study of the Effect of Two Doses of Biosynthetic Human Growth Hormone on Final Height of Children with Familial Short Stature," *Hormone Research* 70, no. 2 (2008): 89–92.

20. Daniel M. Rosen, *Dope: A History of Performance Enhancement in Sports from the Nineteenth Century to Today* (Westport, Conn.: Praeger Publishers, 2008): 75.

21. Macauley, "Doping in Sport," 618.

Chapter 4

1. Shaun Assael, *Steroid Nation* (New York: ESPN Books, 2007): 56–57.

2. Gen Kanayama et al., "Anabolic-androgenic Steroid Dependence: An Emerging Disorder," *Addiction* 104, no. 12 (December 2009): 1966–1978.

3. Clark, *Gladiator,* 234.

Chapter 5

1. Christa Case Bryant, "Floyd Landis Admits Doping to Clear His Conscience, Implicates Lance Armstrong," *Christian Science Monitor*, May 20, 2010, http://www.csmonitor.com/World/Global-News/2010/0520/Floyd-Landis-admits-doping-to-clear-his-conscience-implicates-Lance-Armstrong (accessed December 20, 2010).

2. Petrocelli et al., "Getting Huge, Getting Ripped," 1187–1205.

3. Philippe Tscholl et al., "The Use of Drugs and Nutritional Supplements in Top-Level Track and Field Athletes." *American Journal of Sports Medicine* 38, no. 1 (2009): 133–140.

4. Kuehn, "Teen Steroid, Supplement Use Targeted," 2301–2303.

5. Petrocelli, et al., "Getting Huge, Getting Ripped," 1187–1205.

6. Peter B. Kraska, Charles R. Bussard, and John J. Brent, "Trafficking in Bodily Perfection: Examining the Late-Modern Steroid Marketplace and Its Criminalization," *Justice Quarterly* 27, no. 2 (April 2010): 159–185.

7. National Standard Research Collaboration, "Creatine," Mayo Clinic.com, http://www.mayoclinic.com/health/creatine/NS_patient-creatine (accessed September 12, 2010).

8. U.S. Drug Enforcement Administration (DEA). "DEA Announces Largest Steroid Enforcement Action in U.S. History," *News from DEA*, September 24, 2007, http://www.justice.gov/dea/pubs/pressrel/pr092407.html (accessed September 15, 2010).

Chapter 6

1. Sunny Pepper, " 'Jersey Shore' Buff Ronnie Plagued by Steroid Reports," *Examiner.com*, August 15, 2010, http://www.examiner.com/celebrity-fitness-and-health-in-national/jersey-shore-buff-ronnie-plagued-by-steroid-reports-video (accessed September 10, 2010).

2. "The Situation Worth $5 Million a Year: His Most Ridiculous Endorsements," *Huffington Post*, http://www.huffingtonpost.com/2010/08/23/the-situation-worth-5-mil_n_691241.html (accessed August 23, 2010).

3. Petrocelli et al., "Getting Huge, Getting Ripped," 1187–1205.
4. Associated Press, "China Caught Offering Gene Doping to Athletes," msnbc.com, July 23, 2008, http://www.msnbc.msn.com/id/25816605/ns/beijing_olympics-beijing_olympics_news (accessed January 1, 2011).

Glossary

17-alpha alkylated compounds   a type of steroid that has a higher potential to damage the liver

acne   a skin condition common in steroid users that results from bacteria clogging the skin pores and causing blackheads, whiteheads, and pimples

addiction transference   when a recovering addict develops a new addiction

adrenal glands   triangular-shaped glands that are located above the kidneys and produce a small amount of testosterone along with other hormones

amino acids   the building blocks of protein

anabolic   muscle-building

androgenic   development of secondary male characteristics such as deepening of the voice

androgenic anabolic steroids (AAS)   steroids synthesized from testosterone

anemia   lower levels of red blood cells in the body

anticoagulants   medications that prevent the blood from clotting

autotransfusion   when an athlete withdraws blood and then stores it with the intention of reinjecting it to boost the overall amount of red blood cells in the body

blood pressure   a measurement of the pressure that circulating blood exerts upon the walls of blood vessels

capon   a neutered rooster

cardiomyopathy   weakening of the heart muscle

cholesterol   a waxy steroid molecule that is transported in the blood

chronic kidney disease   a serious condition wherein the kidneys lose their ability to remove wastes and excess water from the body

corticosteroids   steroid hormones used to treat disorders related to inflammation that do not have an anabolic or androgenic effect

creatine   a substance synthesized naturally in the body from amino acids and taken as a supplement to add muscle

designer steroids   synthetic anabolic-androgenic steroids that were created to avoid detection in a drug test

dilated cardiomyopathy   enlarged heart

doping   taking a drug, such as steroids, to enhance athletic performance

ephedra   a plant extract taken as a dietary supplement that stimulates the central nervous system but possesses serious side effects

erythropoietin (EPO)   a hormone that increases red blood cell production

estrogen   female sex hormone produced in the ovaries

eunuch   a castrated man

front-loading   taking a higher drug dosage in the first few days or weeks of usage

gene doping   the transfer of genetic material to improve athletic performance

gynecomastia   the development of breast tissue in males

hemoglobin   a protein responsible for the transporting of oxygen in red blood cells

HIV wasting syndrome   also referred to as AIDS wasting; the loss of more than 10 percent of body weight, plus more than 30 days of diarrhea, weakness, and fever

home brewing   the process of manufacturing AAS or PEDs

human growth hormone (HGH)   a naturally occurring protein-based hormone in the body that is necessary for growth and metabolism

hypertension   occurs when cerebrospinal fluid pressure inside the skull is too high

hypothesis   an educated prediction of the outcome of an experiment

idiopathic short stature   shortness due to genetics rather than pathology

immunosuppression   the suppression of the body's immune system

liver function panel   a blood test that assesses the health of the liver

methandrostenolone (Dianabol)   a popular steroid created by Ciba Pharmaceuticals in 1958 as a preferred alternative to testosterone

nodular acne   acne that originates deeper within the skin layers than normal acne, and that has a high chance of causing scarring

obsessive-compulsive disorder (OCD)   a mental disorder characterized by repetitive behaviors such as repeated hand washing, and other behaviors, including excessive exercise

off-label use   prescribing a drug for a purpose not approved by the FDA

Oral-Turinabol   a favored drug of East Germany's Olympic team in the 1970s and 1980s

osteoporosis   a disease that causes bones to become brittle and fracture easily

out-of-competition testing   an anti-doping strategy where athletes must be available for drug testing whenever it is requested

patellar tendinitis   occurs when the tendon connecting the kneecap to the shinbone is disconnected

PED   *see* performance-enhancing drugs

peliosis hepatis   a serious disease wherein blood-filled cysts form on the liver

performance-enhancing drugs   compounds including, but not limited to, steroids that increase athletic performance through stimulating muscle growth, increasing stamina, or some other biological change

placebo   an inert substance, such as a sugar pill, that is administered to a control group

placebo effect   the tendency of an inert substance (i.e., a placebo) to have a beneficial effect on the recipient simply because he or she believes that it will work

precursor   a chemical that changes into another drug

primary hypogonadism   a condition where the testes produce little or no hormones

Raynaud's syndrome   a chronic condition where a person experiences episodes of decreased circulation in the hands and feet

receptors   protein molecules in the body that are embedded in cells where signaling molecules can attach

red blood cells   main means by which vertebrates deliver oxygen to the body

skeletal muscle   elastic fibers in the body that are responsible for movement and support of the skeleton

stacking   when two or more PEDs are used at the same time

steroid cycle   the number of days the user chooses to take steroids continuously followed by a respite

testosterone   the male sex hormone

tetrahydrogestrinone (THG)   a designer steroid chemically similar to the banned steroids gestrinone and trenbolone; also known as "The Clear"

tissue edema   a condition in which fluid builds up under the skin

transgenic DNA   genetic material that comes from another species

trenbolone   a legal steroid used for cattle, but often sold over the Internet and chemically altered for illegal human consumption

Turner's syndrome   a genetic condition in which a female is lacking an X chromosome

Further Resources

Books and Articles

Bahrke, Michael, and Charles E. Yesalis. *Performance Enhancing Substances in Sport and Exercise*. Champaign, Ill.: Human Kinetics, 2002.

Bayless, Skip. *God's Coach*. Whitby, Ontario: Fireside Publishers, 1991.

Brewer, Benjamin D. "Commercialization in Professional Cycling 1950–2001: Institutional Transformations and the Rationalization of 'Doping.'" *Sociology of Sport Journal* 19, no. 3 (September 2002): 276–300.

Curry, Timothy Jon, and Matthew A. Salerno. "A Comment on the Use of Anabolic Steroids in Women's Olympic Swimming: A Chronicle of the 100-Meters Freestyle." *International Review for the Sociology of Sport* 34, no. 2 (1999): 173–180.

Haggard, Jesse. *Demystifying Steroids*. Bloomington, Ind.: Authorhouse, 2008.

Kiesbye, Stefan. *Steroids*. Farmington Hills, Mich.: Greenhaven Press, 2007.

Mayo Foundation for Medical Education and Research. *Mayo Clinic Book of Alternative Medicine, 2nd ed.* New York: Time, 2010.

Meinhardt, Udo, Anne E. Nelson, Jennifer L. Hansen, Vita Birzniece, David Clifford, Kin-Chuen Leung, Kenneth Graham, and Ken K. Y. Ho. "The Effects of Growth Hormone on Body Composition and Physical Performance in Recreational Athletes: A Randomized Trial." *Annals of Internal Medicine* 152, no. 9 (May 4, 2010): 568–577.

———. "Summaries for Patients: Effects of Growth Hormone Doping on Athletic Performance." *Annals of Internal Medicine* 152, no. 9 (May 4, 2010): I–44.

Monroe, Judy. *Steroids, Sports, and Body Image: The Risks of Performance-Enhancing Drugs*. Berkeley Heights, N.J.: Enslow Publishers, 2004.

Olson, James, M.D. *Clinical Pharmacology Made Ridiculously Simple*. Miami, Fla.: MedMaster, 1995.

Pope, Harrison G., Katharine A. Phillips, and Roberto Olivardia. *The Adonis Complex: The Secret Crisis of Male Body Obsession*. New York: Free Press, 2002.

Solberg, Harry Arne, Dag Vidar Hanstad, and Thor Atle Thøring. "Doping in Elite Sport—Do the Fans Care?" *International Journal of Sports Marketing and Sponsorship* 11, no. 3 (April (2010): 185–199.

Terral, Philippe, Cécile Collinet, and Mathieu Delandre. "A Sociological Analysis of the Controversy over Electric Stimulation to Increase Muscle Strength in the Field of French Sport Science in the 1990s." *International Review for the Sociology of Sport* 44, no. 4 (December 2009): 399–415.

Tscholl, Philippe, Juan M. Alonso, Gabriel Dollé, Astrid Junge, and Jiri Dvorak. "The Use of Drugs and Nutritional Supplements in Top-Level Track and Field Athletes." *American Journal of Sports Medicine* 38, no. 1 (January 2010): 133–140.

Web Sites

Drug Digest
http://www.drugdigest.org

eMedicineHealth
http://www.emedicinehealth.com

KidsHealth
http://kidshealth.org

The Mayo Clinic
http://www.mayoclinic.com

U.S. Food and Drug Administration (FDA)
http://www.fda.gov

WebMD
http://www.webmd.com

World Anti-Doping Agency (WADA)
http://www.wada-ama.org

Index

About the Author

Suellen May writes health and environmental science books, including *Weight-Loss Drugs, Ritalin and Related Drugs, Botox and Other Cosmetic Drugs, Date Rape Drugs,* and a five-volume environmental series titled Invasive Species. She earned a B.S. from the University of Vermont and an M.S. from Colorado State University, and lives in Fort Collins, Colorado, with her son.

About the Consulting Editor

Consulting editor **David J. Triggle, Ph.D.,** is a SUNY Distinguished Professor and the University Professor at the State University of New York at Buffalo. These are the two highest academic ranks of the university. Professor Triggle received his education in the United Kingdom with a Ph.D. degree in chemistry at the University of Hull. Following postdoctoral fellowships at the University of Ottawa (Canada) and the University of London (United Kingdom) he assumed a position in the School of Pharmacy at the University at Buffalo. He served as chairman of the Department of Biochemical Pharmacology from 1971 to 1985 and as Dean of the School of Pharmacy from 1985 to 1995. From 1996 to 2001 he served as Dean of the Graduate School and from 1999 to 2001 was also the University Provost. He is currently the University Professor, in which capacity he teaches bioethics and science policy, and is President of the Center for Inquiry Institute, a think tank located in Amherst, New York, and devoted to issues around the public understanding of science. In the latter respect he is a major contributor to the online M.Ed. program—"Science and The Public"—in the Graduate School of Education and The Center for Inquiry.